Hey! Bartender!

By Johnny Catanio and Patricia Alma Lee

with Amanda Catanio

Cover Credit: Amanda Catanio

ISBN: 145374665X
ISBN-13: 9781453746653

Dedication

For my mother, Antoinetta — the best storyteller I have ever known.

Foreword

By Amanda Catanio

I remember the days when my mother would excitedly announce to my brother and I that grandpa was coming to visit. We were young, roughly five and six years old, those ages when you know who your grandparents are but are confused as to the reason why you have so many. We would look at my mom with childlike charm and ask: Is it papa with the vroom vroom or papa with the batteries? Papa with the vroom vroom she would say… and it was then that we knew our grandfather with his motorcycle and guitar would be on his way to see us.

The most I knew about this man was that he had a voice that charmed and a motorcycle that could be heard down the road. He brought with him the greeting "Where's my most beautiful granddaughter in the whole wide world?" and of course his favorite guitar, on which he would sing to me my very own song "Amanda Sue... I love you."

It wasn't until 2009 that I realized that song wasn't for me, but was for some other woman named "Peggy Sue!" Buddy Holly's famous hit came before my time. With that revelation came many others. It was as if this new man was unfolding before me in the pages of this book. Though difficult to read, and even painful at times, in the end I realized that he is still my grandfather. He is the same man whose love for me has never changed. Joy has come to me in knowing my grandfather for who he was and is and to have spent this time hearing his story.

Disclaimer

My intention is to tell the story of my life -- what I've experienced and what I've learned. I've made an effort to present the truth as I see it. None of what I've written is meant to hurt anyone. I apologize if it does. By the way, some names have been changed – to protect the innocent and the guilty!

Contents

Chapter 1: Golden Dreams

The Golden Dream Cocktail

Serve to very special people at very special events.

1 scoop of vanilla ice cream
1 ounce of white crème de cacao
1 ounce of Galliano
1 ounce of orange juice
1 ounce of heavy cream
1 scoop of ice
Blend until creamy. Pour into martini or champagne glasses. Sprinkle with nutmeg. Serves 2. Enjoy!

A Golden Opportunity

In those awful seconds before the crash, I thought only of how stupid the whole thing was. Here I was at 15 with my buddy, Rashy, in the hottest car ever, a silver-grey 1941 Packard roadster, happily driving along Hudson Boulevard in Jersey City. Suddenly, a Bantam rooster flapped into the front seat, squawking and pooping in our faces.

This did not make for safe driving.

The bird, which had had its legs tied, had been resting quietly on the car's back seat floor. We'd bought him at a North Bergen live poultry market as a gift for a friend and he'd been so quiet we'd forgotten about him. Then, when we turned a sharp corner, he had been thrown across the car, woken up and decided to fight for his life.

In those seconds with the flapping rooster in his face, Rashy couldn't see. He rear-ended another car that was stopping for a red light. On impact, my head and the windshield collided and the windshield won (no seatbelts back then). I was a bloody mess. The blood gushed from a deep cut on my forehead. A motorcycle cop, who appeared out of nowhere, looked us over and determined quickly that none of us involved in the accident had life-threatening injuries. I was particularly glad about that as I had no idea how badly hurt I was or wasn't! Then, apparently feeling big brotherly, the cop took me aside and told me what I should do.

"First", he said, "Go to the emergency room and get the care you need. Second, call this attorney. (He handed me a business card.) You should be able to get something out of this."

What was he saying? Being somewhat innocent, I told him that there was no way I could sue my friend for damages. Rashy had sponsored me when I was confirmed as a Catholic. He was my pal and I admired him. No way! The officer patiently explained that I would be suing Rashy's insurance company – not him directly.

On the way to the ER, I attempted to explain this plan to my buddy, a hot-tempered Sicilian. He blew up. Such emotion! He was wounded to the core. It even crossed my mind that our friendship might end. After much persuasion he calmed down, though. (It probably helped when I told him I intended to share any money I received from the insurance company with him.) We stayed friends.

I had other buddies, too. With four prior years of diligent coaching by Bob Martin, I did especially well in high school gymnastics. I, and my neighborhood friends, Tony Calamito, Ludwig Birdman, and Billy Lee, made up the first gymnastics team from Ferris High School to win both Jersey City and New Jersey State championships. Coach Martin confided to me that I could probably get a scholarship to college if I wanted to go. That sounded good to me. This concept of my future didn't last very long, though. When I got up the courage to say I was interested in going to college, my parents said flatly I couldn't be in school when money was needed at home.
Dad worked for a coal company that transported coal by barge from the Jersey City docks to the various boroughs of New York. Just his one salary to support 10 people wasn't nearly enough.

Being the eldest, I had a responsibility to help our family financially. I felt it keenly. Of course, my parents were right, I thought. Be practical.
Soon after that, I quit high school. I had too much going on anyway: studying, helping with my brothers and sisters, work, and gymnastics practice. I couldn't juggle it all -- something had to go. OK. My school days were over. My immediate future would be as a wage earner for our family.

So, with my tenth grade education I offered myself to the world of work. My menial jobs included sales and service in a chicken market, driving a bakery truck, and working as a shuttler in the embroidery industry. The shuttler job included long hours and good pay and I soon earned more than my father. With my salary, too, conditions at home improved. We ate better dinners with meat instead of the usual vegetable soup or pasta. Desserts and soft drinks appeared as occasional treats. That year, all my brothers and sisters got really nice Christmas gifts. They all considered me a sort of god.

Two years passed in a blur. One life-changing day, my parents went with me to the settlement hearing about the car accident at the Jersey City Courthouse on Newark Avenue. They had to attend. I was still a minor and they were required to sign a release. During the hearing, I was awarded a check for three thousand dollars. I knew what I wanted to do with it: make my mother happy.

That money became the down payment for a nice house for our family in the Greenville section of town. From the tenement in downtown Jersey City, where few opportunities existed, we moved to a good neighborhood — safer, cleaner, with better schools for my younger brothers and sisters. This was big!

So my mother's golden dream came true when we bought a house. That was what she had always wanted. I was happy for her and proud that I could help. The fulfillment of my golden dream, though, would have to wait quite a while.

Chapter 2:
My Mother,
Antoinetta

Eight Plus One

When I was growing up, my seven younger siblings and I invented our own ways of having fun. We did this mostly because we had to. We just didn't have the entertainment options of today. Computers, videos, TV, cell phones -- these inventions came later. For example, my family got our first TV when I was 15. We had to be creative and learn to entertain ourselves: our parents were busy. Still, in our family, my mother, Antoinetta, was our best entertainer.

My mother was born in Rochester, New York. Her mother, Camilla, died suddenly of pneumonia when Antoinetta was two. By then, there were a total of three daughters and one son in that family -- my mother being the youngest. After his wife's death, Antoinetta's father, Corrado, a tree surgeon, couldn't take care of his family without the help of his relatives who lived in Italy. He moved back to his farm in Pisticii, a small town located in the instep of the Italian boot. For her growing up years, Antoinetta De Pinto held onto the knowledge that she was an American citizen. She yearned to return to the U.S., known as the land of opportunity. When she was 18 she did move back with her sister, Isabella, and Isabella's husband, Paul.

Mother's stories of growing up on a farm without running water, electricity, and indoor plumbing struck us as if she had lived in the Middle Ages! After all, we were city kids. Mother told us about taking care of animals, riding horses, and having to walk to fetch water from a well for drinking and washing.

She hadn't gone to school herself, so when I went to school and learned to read and write, I brought home my books and taught her. She made the firm decision that only English would be spoken in our home. I remember she and my father had strong disagreements about this. I often wonder why we didn't grow up speaking both English and Italian. Was it because mother didn't think during that time it would be wise to be speaking the language of one of our enemies in the War? Or was it because she wanted us to learn English quickly and fit in faster? I still puzzle over it.

The day she could write her own name in English was thrilling for both of us. Sadly, my father chided my mother, instead of encouraging her, as she struggled to make progress reading and writing in English. He enjoyed embarrassing her. I guess it made him feel more powerful.

Despite my father's bouts of heavy drinking, we were often a happy family. The personal fears we faced were mostly of my father becoming drunk and then turning violent and beating my mother. As best I could, I looked out for her when these episodes happened. I was especially close to my mother. She loved me unconditionally and I felt she needed my protection.

The bigger fears about the war and what was happening in the world at large became especially real when our neighbor boys left for military duty. We knew them well and the goodbyes were sad and scared us. Warning sirens shrieking in our neighborhood and all the lights going out (blackouts) is another memory. My mother would call us in from the street and gather us under the kitchen table (for protection!) and pray out loud to God for our safety. I have to say that my earliest memories are those of fear. I was five when WWII began and 10 when it ended.

I remember sitting in Miss Kennedy's art class in third grade daydreaming about warmth and sunshine. My art works at that time depicted the same scene repeatedly; a beach sandscape with coconut palms and saw grass bending in the breeze. Sleek sailboats with stick figures on board, heeled over in response to the wind on the blue, blue water, in the background.

Don't ask which color of blue I used though, because I'm partially color blind and couldn't tell you. I remember clearly being in a panic because sometimes Miss Kennedy would call on me to bring her a ream of a specific color of paper from the storage cabinet to distribute to the class for that day's art project. I didn't want my classmates to know that I couldn't tell one color from another. That would have made me look stupid. Thomas, the class prig, figured out I felt this way and would charge me 10 cents to tell me which color she wanted so I'd get it right!

I vowed that one day when I was grown up I would get out of Jersey City -- that God-forsaken place -- and move to Miami. I wanted out of the dark, cold, slush and into the bright, warm, sunshine. That was my golden dream.

Our lives weren't all misery and daydreams. We got joy from simple pleasures like singing. My mother loved to sing as I do. One of her favorites that she sang to me was: "Oh, Johnny, Johnny, Oh!" a popular WW I song written by Ed Rose and Abe Oleman in 1917. The song became popular again in the 1940s. Here are the words.

"Oh, Johnny! Oh, Johnny!
How you can love!
Oh, Johnny! Oh, Johnny!
Heavens above!
You make my sad heart jump with joy,
And when you're near I just can't sit still a minute,
I'm so, Oh, Johnny! Oh, Johnny!
Please tell me dear,
What makes me love you so?
You're not handsome it's true,
But when I look at you,
I just Oh! Johnny!
Oh, Johnny! Oh!"

Other songs I remember she sang to us were "You Are My Sunshine," and "Return to Sorrento."

One of the popular ditties at this time among us kids, was:
"Whistle while you work,
Hitler is a jerk,
Mussolini is a meanie,
But the Japs are worse!"

13

My next younger brother, nicknamed Cocoa, was 18 months younger than me but about the same size. He could be wild and we often got into it. As a group, we older kids made up puppet shows using family members as thinly disguised characters. We also attempted magic tricks. Somehow we thought we should be able to do imitations as well, so Cocoa and I practiced doing Al Jolsen and competed with each other to be the best. We also took the younger ones to the nearby playground and tried to make sure the bruises and broken bones were minimal.

My mother could be very funny, and one of her lines was "I only had sex with my husband 8 times!" Of course, that's the number of children they had together. Following mine, these are the names of each of my brothers and sisters in order of their birth and their ages when I was 15.

The Catanio Siblings

Johnny (Giovanni): 15
Cocoa (Corrado): 13
Mario: 11
Paul: 10
Camille: 8
Maryanne: 4
Anthony: 2
Richard: just born!

We paired off in twos – we each were buddies with the next younger child. By the way, my father named every child but the last one. Actually we got another one, but she arrived with her own name. Eight children, were not enough for my mother. She adopted Nancy, a five-year-old girl from Italy, who'd been brought to the U.S. by one of our relatives. The relative hadn't been able to bear any children and had hoped to raise this little girl but couldn't handle her bad behavior. My mother took Nancy in with us when she'd almost been sent back to Italy. Mother wouldn't hear of that. She understood what Nancy's life would be like – she'd lived there -- so Nancy settled in with us. Mother was the most loving woman I've ever known. She used her hard-won experience, careful attention, and discipline and soon loved Nancy into better behavior.

The relatives from both sides of our family visited our house at least a couple times a month. Both my father and mother were the youngest – the babies – in their large families so they were considered special.

My mother had a card game she would play with us after the relatives had come over and given us coins during their visit. This is one of my very earliest memories. She called it "Pots" and with her accent it came out "Pot-sa." She would call us all together and announce: "It's-a time-a for a little game of pot-sa!"

We'd be excited about the possibility of winning "big" money. She'd shuffle the cards and make five even piles called "pots." We would choose a pot by putting the coins on top of it. The object was to have your card at the bottom of the pile turn out to be higher than the one at the bottom of the dealer's pile (which was Mom's). She always won. We didn't feel too bad though because she used her winnings to make us home-made pizzas – 6 to 8 large ones – and invited the neighbor kids to come over and eat, too. Antoinetta gained a neighborhood reputation for her generosity and her home-made pizzas.

Antoinetta did a mean imitation of Chubby Checkers doing the twist. Mother was roly-poly and she really went at it. Talk about a spectacle!

In her later years, when I would visit her in New Jersey, we'd sit and talk. She told me that when she was asked about why I'd had so many wives, she would say: "Because Johnny always marries his girlfriends." Antoinetta is the only woman in my life who truly loved me unconditionally.

My mother spent the last couple years of her life talking out loud to God about anything and everything. Her children provided for her so she could stay in her own home, her wish. She died when she was 86.

I seldom go home to Jersey City any more.

Chapter 3: My First Love, Marion

My Bardot

Marion, my first love, a beautiful woman, who I loved dearly – the mother of my three sons -- died in 2005. Her last dying wish was to have her sons around her. Sadly, that didn't happen.

I was 19 and Marion was 15 when we talked at a first communion party held for one of her cousins. Actually, I had seen her once when she was 12 and she affected me so strongly I got light-headed! She resembled Bridget Bardot and used it to her advantage. What attitude! It drew me even more. Marion had a sister who was my age and attended the same classes with me at school.

In those days, I would have to describe myself as shy, occasionally friendly, and reckless – of course my recklessness increased with the drinking I did.

We married too young. After I had been away for military training and returned on a leave from the Army we married. She had sent me several photos of herself that left little to the imagination and was threatening not to wait for me unless I married her so I did.

She was a jealous person and had a short temper. I don't remember her ever being like this until after we married. Often when we drank together, our behavior got very ugly. Because she knew that I would never get violently physical with her, she taunted me and often hit me. When I saw "The Godfather," the movie so popular in the U.S. in the 60s, the female character who played Mike's sister, reminded me of Marion.

Hey! Bartender!

For years, we thought her father was Albanian, but the fact was that he was from a town called Albanese in Italy. We laughed when we learned this because Pisticii, where my mother was from, is in the same region.

Marion and I shared 10 years, had three children together – all boys -- and were divorced when I was 31. We were living in Houston, Texas at that time. I went home to Jersey City to be consoled by my mother, I was so sad and bewildered. I'll tell you more about that later.

Chapter 4: Early Exposures

Electrical Connections

One of my first "real" jobs was as a technician at Western Electric assembling circuit boards on a production line. I was called in to Mr. Buhler's office one day. I wondered what was up because he was my supervisor and private meetings like this were unusual. After briefly discussing my work with me, he asked: "Do you read newspapers and books?"

"No, I don't," I replied honestly.

I couldn't tell if he was insulting me or actually trying to help me.

Although, I respected him, I was young, suspicious, and emotionally touchy. He told me reading was a great way to learn about the world. He said I didn't have to go to college to learn new things. I took that conversation to heart. Soon afterward, I became an avid and prolific reader and discovered I especially liked philosophy, psychology, and history. His advice changed my life for the better.

I went to a trade school for electrical engineering and found the required math courses challenging. I found that I could do the work and the pay was good so that was OK with me. Later, however, when I apprenticed in the hospitality industry at the Walburn Hotel, I found the work that I truly loved.

During the time I was working at Western Electric, they began layoffs. It was then that I decided it was a ripe time to join the Army – I could get a bonus and credit and the promise of a job when I returned from service.

I signed up.

Hey! Bartender!

Previously, as a shy seventeen-year-old, I had joined the National Guard and went to weekly meetings and camp twice a year for three years. I was nearly 21 when I volunteered for the Army. It was February and I was freezing my ass off in Fort Dix, New Jersey, at the Army Induction Center. I really hoped they wouldn't order me to take basic training there because I was sure I would freeze to death. Happily, they didn't. Instead, I was ordered to Fort Benning, Georgia to take basic training with the Third Infantry Division. That was the furthest South I'd ever been. All you needed to wear outside was a light jacket — even in winter. I hadn't ever been away from home that long, either. They kept us really busy, but I was still lonely.

Sooner than it seemed possible, I'd successfully completed the first eight weeks of basic training. I had a regular salary. I loved Marion and wanted to be with her. It was all so simple! So, we got married. I was 21 and she was 17. Our first son, named after me but nicknamed Jay, was conceived at Fort Benning, Georgia.

After a year, I was transferred from Fort Benning to Fort Bragg, North Carolina. I was lucky with my military service. They continued my electronics training. The only "action" I ever saw while serving my country was cracking heads when I played running back in football for the Third Infantry Division!

Since I'd been lucky so far, I thought I'd get out while the gettin' was good. I did.

Chapter 5:
Hava Nagila

I Find My True Work

Years passed. Marion and I had terrible fights followed by short separations. Then we'd weaken and get back together – telling ourselves it was best for the boys.

The final drama was Christmas 1965 when we stopped at my mother's house to deliver gifts. We argued, tempers flared, and Marion slapped me across the face in front of mother. I calmly left the scene. I drove back to our house, packed and started driving south to a new beginning.

I drove and drove until I saw a sign that read: "Welcome to Florida: The Sunshine State." I drove on until I reached Miami and then Miami Beach. This was late December, it was sunny and 85 degrees. I was startled by people with white hair playing tennis or out walking. I'd never seen active seniors like these. At home the older people I knew sat around in wheelchairs complaining about the cold weather. My golden dream and the fountain of youth had been rolled into one!

After hours of sight-seeing, I drove back to the mainland. I got a room at the Vagabond Motel on Biscayne Street. Then I bought a Miami Herald and began scanning the classifieds for a job.

Working at the Walburn

When Jack Schwartz, the general manager of the Walburn Hotel, interviewed me, I sold myself to him by saying I would work for free for a week. After that he could decide whether or not I was the right person for the job. I'd had no hotel experience. What I did have was some experience managing rental properties so I had lots of building repair and maintenance skills.

Hey! Bartender!

Jack had read aloud the varied and lengthy list of job tasks, probably thinking I would get discouraged, but I thought I could handle them. Mainly, they included managing the wait-staff and bus boys during the three-meal-a-day kosher food service and performing the front desk activities – like registering guests and operating the switchboard. Some evenings, the job required entertaining the guests by running bingo games and showing old movies. And, oh, yes!, the person chosen for the job would need to fill in when the bus boys or other help didn't show up for work. I got the job.

* * *

"Johnny! What's for dinner tonight?" Mrs. Goldstein asked between mouthfuls of her lunch. The way she vigorously stabbed at her salad scared me. You'd have thought the woman hadn't eaten in days.

"The chef mentioned Salisbury steak," I said. "That's your favorite entrée, isn't it? I'll get you a large portion." Mrs. Goldstein smiled briefly and then once again concentrated fully on stabbing and eating.

Her friend, Shellie, patted her on the shoulder. "Good to have Johnny looking out for you." One of the true sweethearts of the place, Shellie had been on my side since day one, when I helped her and Mrs. Goldstein move their belongings into another room on a different floor. I wouldn't accept any tip from them – just told them that they'd been inconvenienced enough and I was happy to help out. The pipes in their bathroom had leaked and they'd both been very upset about having to change rooms. For years since their husbands had died, they had stayed in the same room together because they said they liked the view. Later, I came to know the real reason. They liked being next door to their late husbands' guy friends. After they played cards with them until all hours, they could both just toddle next door and collapse on their beds.

OK. Did you like that story about Mrs. Goldstein? I just made that up but in fiction there's truth. The story expresses just what it was like there. Now let's get back to the facts, Jack.

* * *

By the third working day, I already knew the outlines of the personalities and food preferences of many of the guests. Some were very demanding characters – shouting orders as if they were generals. Others complained about the coffee not being hot enough, or the vegetables being overcooked, or the room temperature being too cold. All –without exception – enjoyed attention. The people staying at the Walburn were orthodox Jews in later life whose middle-aged children had placed them there, away from the snow and cold, for the winter months. These months included November through Passover in April. Their children often stayed with their own spouses and families at the Fountainbleu – Eden Rock Hotels. This arrangement meant that they were close enough to visit their parents yet far enough away to be able to enjoy themselves more freely.

Another wonderful man, my friend during the three years I worked there, was a guest named Joe Finkelstein. He was in his 80s when we met – tall, with beautiful, bright, blue eyes and a craggy face full of lines and furrows. He would get two gratis tickets to the Friday night wrestling matches and the weekly taping of the Jackie Gleason show and bring me along as his companion. His granddaughter was married to the producer of the Jackie Gleason show, the biggest TV hit at that time, and this was their weekly gift to him (and me)! Did we have fun!

Before landing this job, remember, I had worked as an electrician. Although it was a good job in many ways, this experience taught me that I was meant for the hospitality industry – not electrical work. The benefits of working at the Walburn were that I could eat and stay there, occupancy permitting, as part of my work arrangement. Then I could send most of the money I earned home to Marion and the boys. Plus, I just loved the work!

Jose's Brothers

"It's just not like Jose. He didn't show up and he didn't call," I said to Jack. Annoyed at being caught off guard, we were both hustling to fill in because besides Jose not showing, we'd had other waiters at the Walburn call in sick. With nearly a hundred people to serve at breakfast, lunch, and dinner, we couldn't afford for meal crew members to be late – much less not come in. Our strict rules about lateness and time off had been pretty effective – until today.

Hey! Bartender!

Jose, our only Cuban, (nearly every ethnic mix imaginable was employed there) had worked at the hotel as a waiter since our season had begun in late October. It was now January. In Cuba, his family had owned and operated a jewelry business and he had younger brothers still living there. He worked really hard to be able to send money home. Polite, attentive and mild-mannered, he earned good tips – even from those who were tight with a dollar. I knew his own family included a wife and a young daughter and son. I'd just seen their photos.

I asked around that morning's breakfast crew to see what they knew about his situation and learned nada. Even the man he sometimes rode to work with hadn't seen him since the day before. As the hours passed and we still hadn't heard from him, I worried that he'd been in an accident. Although providing breakfast service and the prep for lunch kept us really busy, in the back of my mind I wondered what had happened to him. He had an owner's work ethic – be on time, be reliable, be good to people, work hard – so I knew it had to be something serious.

Finally, Jose arrived just before lunch. As I was ready to lay into him, he cut me off with a sharp look. With tears in his eyes he said: "Castro shot my three brothers yesterday! They were executed by firing squad!" In disbelief, I hugged him though I really didn't know how to begin to console him. I remember that I said some words about how sorry I was for him and his family. They sounded perfunctory. None of us knew what to do or say.

"My duty is clear," he said. "I will take revenge in whatever way I can. This is now my purpose. Good-bye my friends." He left abruptly. The whole interaction had taken less than five minutes. I sat down with the others, stunned into silence. His friends among the women were crying softly and the men were stone-faced and uncomfortable. The usual chattiness among us as lunch was served and eaten was replaced by an eerie respectful silence.

As the news spread about Jose's brothers, we all wondered what kind of crazy world we were living in.

Chapter 6: Adventures with Lum's

On the Move

This back and forth between Jersey City and Miami was wearing me out and putting our family back together became a priority for Marion and me.

I had worked at the Walburn Hotel in-season (winter) and then went home to Jersey City and worked there (sort of) doing construction and repair odd jobs. I still lived with Marion and the boys during the hotel's off-season. Mostly, my three boys were growing up without me and it pained me. I missed them. I also felt guilty – like I wasn't being a good father to them. If we didn't have our meddling families close by and interfering in our struggles, I thought Marion, the boys, and I could make it together. At this stage, I couldn't see that my behavior was a major part of our problem. Talk about denial! Marion and I talked it over and decided we'd try having everyone live in Florida fulltime.

First, everybody had to get there. That drive of more than 1,350 miles, in a car without air conditioning, was a nightmare never to be forgotten. The boys, aged 8, 6, and 4, screamed, fought, and cried along the way – that is when they weren't asking for a stop to pee or buy candy. I remember barking at Marion because she couldn't maintain order in the back seat. The games we'd thought of to play kept the boys occupied only briefly – like 5 seconds! – before we had to create other diversions. We drove during the daylight hours. We wanted to see as much as we could as we rolled along. Also, safety ranked high with us. Since Marion didn't have a driver's license, I was the only driver. At night, we chose motels with swing sets and pools so the boys could have fun and wear themselves out. After a good night's sleep though, they'd be as rowdy as ever the next morning. Confining them in a car for hours was torture for them – and for us!

After I made a few idle threats to drop them off in the middle of nowhere if they didn't shape up, which they didn't find funny, we finally arrived in Miami. We stayed at Ester's rooming house, where I'd stayed often before, while we searched for an adequate apartment. Soon, we found a four-room cottage near Miami Shores on North East 88th Street. Tucked behind the main house, where our landlady, Mrs. Whitney, and her family lived, we felt safe and a part of the neighborhood. In the year that we lived there, Mrs. Whitney was kind and accommodating.

While interviewing for a fulltime, year-round position, since the seasonal schedule at the Walburn didn't work for our family any more, I found a promising lead. I could be an assistant manager in a family-owned, start-up, fast-food restaurant. I was lured with the promise of a quick promotion to manager if all went well. A new, popular, local store called Lum's was opening a few new locations in Dade and Broward counties. Brothers Stuart and Clifford Perlman were growing Lum's and I thought their concept was a winner. Keep the menu simple: high quality hot dogs boiled in beer. Execute well: provide quick and friendly service. Franchising was just beginning to take off in the food business at this time. Their first Lum's location was in a converted garage in Miami Beach across the street from the very famous Forge Restaurant on 41st Street.

From this solo hot dog stand that the Perlman's purchased for about $20,000 (the figure quoted varies) they grew their business to 400 stores and a listing on the NY Stock Exchange. They then sold the entire enterprise and became wealthy. Next, they bought a casino in Las Vegas and turned it into another huge business success: Caesar's World, a highly profitable gaming empire.

As luck would have it, they assigned me to help operate one of the busiest locations they had – adjacent to the Miami airport on 36th Street. We were across from the Eastern Airlines section of the terminal. As a newcomer, you are often able to observe what others may miss. What I saw was this: certain waitresses were pocketing tickets and cash in their aprons after collecting it at the end of providing service. Part of that collected cash never made it to the cashier because they thought no one was watching. After seeing this happen repeatedly, I reported the scam to a person above the level of my immediate boss, who was the store manager. (I did that because I wasn't sure if he was in on the scam or not.)

The upshot was several waitresses were fired, the store manager was reprimanded for not monitoring his staff more closely, and I got a reward. The North Miami store got a new Italian-American store manager named Johnny.

Sadly, Marion's and my rosy idea of making our family life work didn't take very long to unravel. My career with Lum's was taking off and I was working long hours and enjoying the challenges. I also liked working with the pretty, young waitresses I managed and Marion became jealous. She kept telling me she wanted me to get back to electrical construction work: "a real man's job" as she put it. Once in a while, she would make an unannounced visit to check up on me at the restaurant. She was drinking heavily at the time and would create terrible scenes. These left me angry and embarrassed in front of my staff and customers. It just couldn't continue.

So, this explains why, when I was offered the chance to be a field representative and travel nationwide to train new Lum's franchise operators, I immediately went for it. My reasoning was that I knew I'd be a success, plus Marion couldn't harass me as much if I was on the road. In addition, the promotion included a pay upgrade and an expense account. All positives! I hit the road.

My co-rep and I first went to Alton, Illinois to work with a young entrepreneur from Florissant, Missouri. He wined and dined us at restaurants in St. Louis and we helped plan and hire staff for his Lum's franchise Spring grand opening. After work, we saw Busch Stadium and the famous "Arch." We marveled at the Alton Locks, located where the Missouri and Mississippi meet, and saw the site of the historic Lincoln-Douglas debate. The three of us were excited about the new store and we were on schedule. We were pretty proud of ourselves.

Then, a few days prior to the opening, we had surprise visitors. Officials from the local restaurant union were milling around out in front of our new site. Two men were even picketing in front of our beautiful, about-to-open store. I had to do something – and quick!

I decided to take the face-to-face approach. I walked out the store's front door and went over to them. I introduced myself and asked what the problem was. They didn't want to do business in the open air and invited me to their nearby office for talks. I agreed and was walked over to a shabby office with a few sticks of furniture, a phone, and a refrigerator filled with beer. First, beers were passed around.

"Did you know you've been hiring non-union personnel and offering below-scale wages?" The head guy, said to me. "One of the women you hired as a waitress is a friend of mine," he added. "She told me."

I listened for a while to the union rates they quoted. They made other demands related to working conditions. After listening for longer than I'm built to, the situation became pretty clear. If we wanted to co-exist peaceably and profitably in the community, we would have to go along and be a union shop.

After some more back and forth, and more beer, I proposed that if they'd remove the pickets and let the franchise open on time we'd meet their requests. They agreed and we shook hands to seal the deal. Then, of course, we had more beer.

Now I had to figure out how to inform the franchisee about the increased costs he'd immediately be incurring. Since he was especially eager to be on good terms with the business people in his new city, I needn't have worried. When I told him what they expected from him, he listened. We decided the simplest approach to offsetting the required increases would be to raise the cost of every item on the menu by 10 cents. We changed the menus, had them reprinted, and opened the doors to the first Lum's franchise in Illinois. Because our team opened the store on time, with fanfare, and despite obstacles, the home office was definitely pleased.

Adventures with Lum's

While traveling with Lum's, I got to see more of the U.S. From Cheektowaga, New York, near Buffalo, I saw the Canadian Niagara Falls and was treated to a memorable Buffalo Bill versus Oakland Raiders game. Buffalo lost 55 to 0 – yes, you read that right– and their coach, Bob Collins was fired. Later that day, by chance, we met Daryl La Monica, the Raiders quarterback, and "The Tree" Henderson at a downtown pub. In Greensboro, North Carolina, I visited my first rathskeller (historically a German bar in the basement of the town hall where important people drink and discuss events of the day) and in East Cleveland, Ohio, I briefly appreciated the frozen beauty of Lake Erie. Despite the dazzling ice and snow, I was reminded once again of how I hate the cold!

When I wasn't on the road, I operated out of the main office at 5050 Biscayne Boulevard in Miami. One of my duties was to drive Ben, Stu and Cliff's father, a retired dentist, when any of them needed a lift. The brothers had many of their relatives working for them – Lum's had a family atmosphere for good reason! Early on, as the business was growing, family members were given stock shares and options which later, when the business succeeded, made them rich.

After a year of travel and several successful Lum's franchise openings, my next adventure came along. One day I arrived at the home office and my boss, also named Johhny, let me know I was being considered for store manager at a Lum's store in Houston. The franchisee had backed out after the store had been made ready for its opening. The potential for becoming an owner if I managed it well was offered and the company would pay moving expenses. OK, then!

Houston had held a place in my heart and my imagination for years before this. An avid fan of Dean Martin as a teenager, I emulated him. (Yes. I even combed my hair like his.) Beyond that, I memorized the words, his mannerisms, and singing style for most of his hits including "Houston."

That became our theme song as we packed up to move and rented out our house in North Miami Beach. Marion and our three sons were as excited as I was. The boys dreamed of horses in their future.

I did buy the cowboy hat and boots. I also proudly displayed an American flag out front, and began running the store. My brother, Paul, worked as night manager for us and Marion worked in the store as well. One of our waitresses also helped babysit the boys.

We explored Old Houston and New Houston driving the loop around the city center that made car travel so easy. Of course, we had to locate the best Italian restaurant immediately and discovered it was New York Pizza, owned by a six–foot–three American-Italian, with a Texas drawl. We all found this combination pretty funny.

The business people and our neighbors in Houston seemed genuinely friendly and I was convinced that Texas had a monopoly on beautiful women. (Not this again!) Marion was still her jealous self and our same old problems began resurfacing. It turns out when you move somewhere, you take your problems along with you...

One afternoon, we did enjoy free tickets to a Houston Astros versus San Francisco Giants baseball game courtesy of our new beer distributor. Our private box seats in the Astro Dome came with wait service (Busch beer for us; popcorn and soda for the boys). Seeing Willie Mays play baseball that day fulfilled a childhood dream for me and because it was "bat day" each of my sons received a free bat. Was this heaven, or what?

Well, it wasn't. Not too long into this adventure, Marion took it upon herself to call the president of Lum's, Stu Perlman, and rant to him about my failings. She claimed I was mistreating her and neglecting the franchise rules. When she'd done this before, my boss, named Johnny, too, had intercepted the calls, listened, and somehow calmed her down. This time though, she accomplished her end: she got through to Stu and got me fired.

I only became aware of this several days later. Surprise! Two company representatives appeared at our store to inform me I was being relieved of my duties due to what Marion had told Mr. Perlman. Angry doesn't begin to describe how I felt. I'd say devastated, humiliated, and broken would be the short list. How could she have done this to me and our family!

During the nasty confrontation with Marion afterward, she explained to me that everything happens for the best. She had decided that I could now return to a real man's job in electrical construction (like I'd had before).

I left immediately and flew home to momma in New Jersey. I vowed never again to be in the same state with my wife. This time, Marion and I were through.

Johnny Guitar

"Everybody loves somebody sometime, everybody falls in love sometime…" I sang. To my ears, I sounded just like Dean Martin himself. Surely my favorite Dean Martin hit would grab 'em. I'd be a paid singer after this audition and who knew where that might lead? I was at Lou's Corner Lounge in Union City, New Jersey. I was pretty excited.

Well, they hired me – for two weekends. My first professional gig earned me $100 plus tips. My repertoire consisted of 12 songs that I'd learned in the three months I'd been staying with mother after separating from Marion. The music soothed my hurt and gave me a positive focus as I slowly recovered emotionally. Besides, everybody knows playing the guitar makes you a chick magnet…

I had a problem when I sang sometimes. I'd first begun singing in piano bars after I reached the legal drinking age and the bands I attempted to sing with sometimes didn't play the songs in my keys. Were they intentionally messing with me? I wondered. Some time afterward, I figured out that many of the musicians didn't know how to transpose into another key. I do think sometimes they were giving the kid who was so full of himself "the business" as well. Whatever. I wasn't 19 any more.

I decided on a solution. I'd learn some simple guitar chords and accompany myself. Having taken clarinet lessons as a child, I had a little music background. So when the time was ripe, I was now in my mid-thirties and looking for a boost after the split from Marion and the boys, I bought an inexpensive guitar. I also bought a few learning books and song sheets and began my crooning career.

Since I worked nights, I practiced during the day for hours, which drove my mother insane. She'd actually run to get out of the house and away from the repetition of the same chords and mistakes. My brother, Cocoa's 10 year-old-son, Frankie, who was taking guitar lessons then, taught me the "Guitar Boogie" and I still play it.

Hey! Bartender!

Often, I sat in with some of the musicians at the restaurants where I worked. I remember very well the night world-class performer, Elvis Presley, died. He and I were about the same age and I didn't know anyone who didn't think he was terrific. Working at Arthur's Eating House that night, Steve, a great pianist, had been playing show tunes. I asked him if I could dedicate a song to Elvis, dead at age 42. I sang "My Way."

Not everyone thrilled to my singing performances at first. At the Goldcoast Restaurant, I sang and Ernie, a manager who worked there, said "Oh shit. A singing bartender – just what we need." When my friends came out to hear me and business in the Cuttysark Lounge picked up, partly due to my singing, his tune changed. He admitted to me privately that he'd been wrong – my singing was an asset.

Singing and playing the guitar have become part of me. After 40-plus years of practice, I've gotten better!

My Favorite Songs
1. "Everybody Loves Somebody Sometime" sung by Dean Martin
2. "Play Me" sung by Neil Diamond
3. "My Way" sung by Frank Sinatra
4. "I Left My Heart In San Francisco" sung by Tony Bennett
5. "Hotel California" sung by The Eagles
6. "Monday, Monday" sung by the Mamas and Papas
7. "The Last Dance" and "New York, New York" sung by Frank Sinatra. These two songs signaled the end of my night shift at Stefano's for many of the years I worked there. When they started playing, I knew I'd survived another crazy, busy night.

My first music books for guitar were by these groups.
1. The Beatles
2. The Mammas and Papas
3. Peter, Paul, and Mary

I liked them because the chords were simple and I could play many of their songs right away!

Chapter 7: Short-Term Gigs

A Bartender's Secret

His admission rocked me. I knew that Joseph was gay. That wasn't it. He was open about his partner, who was a young, black guy – Joseph was white. Other coworkers at Arthur's Eating House teased him about their relationship. Not me, though; I never did.

No. This was something else entirely.

He confided one busy work night that before he had come to Miami he had led a very different life. Once he told me about it, I just had to ask him all kinds of questions. He looked me full in the face and announced that he had been a Catholic priest. Caught by surprise, I laughed and said "This is the first time I've worked BEHIND the bar with a priest!" He laughed, too. Then, I blurted: "Why did you leave the priesthood?"

"The hypocrisy finally became too much," he said. "So many of my fellow clergy were gay and living double lives."

"Really?" I hadn't known this was commonplace. I'd just never given it much thought, I guess. "May I ask you something else?" I said. "It's even more personal."

"Sure."

"How do you maintain your relationship with God, now?" I asked. For the full effect, picture the two of us talking about God in the frenzied environment of a hot, singles restaurant/bar/club with the music pulsing and up so loud you had to shout to be heard.

Rather than shout out a brief answer, he quietly said: "I'll be right back." It was slow at the bar just then. He slipped out from behind it and walked purposefully out of Arthur's front entrance into the parking lot. When he came back, he returned with a book. Smiling, he handed it to me.

"This tells the story better than I ever could," Joseph said. "You'll learn a lot about me if you read it."

So, the next day I put my usual chores aside and read it. The book told about a Christian man living in California who came to a stunning realization in mid-life: he was gay. He had denied it for his whole life until then. After growing up, becoming a minister, getting married, and having children he'd finally faced it. He'd had some early feelings that, had he been open to them, would have revealed the truth about his sexuality. As a minister's son, though, the deep shame of being gay in his family blocked the knowledge from him. When he met another man whom he truly loved and wanted to spend his life with, the full fabric of his life fell apart. Most of his family and friends disowned him. Since he believed that God still loved him, he founded a church for gays and lesbians. Joseph now worshiped in that very church.

I should add that Joseph and his partner impressed me. Both were educated, personable, and handsome. Hardworking Joseph could easily handle practically any role in the restaurant. Of course, his versatility made him a highly valued employee. Another plus, he was sincere and good with people. Since my conversation with Father Joe that night and having read the book he gave me, I understand the gay community better. Before then, I had very little insight into their issues. A sincere thank-you to Father Joe for making me a broader person.

One shift while I was working at Arthur's Eating House in North Miami, Joe Sonken came by with some friends to check me out as a possible hire. Joe was a well-known businessman – older than me, short, stocky cigar-chomping and I never saw him without his trademark longshoreman's cap. That very day, he made me an offer I couldn't refuse so I gave Max notice. I joined Joe's staff at the Goldcoast Restaurant in Hollywood Beach. The switch in environments was from North Miami high-end country club to high-end vacationer's casual. Some regular dining customers drove their boats up and tied them at the dock before coming in. This restaurant definitely had the cool factor. Street signs from Chicago were hung in the parking lot as a welcome to the many visiting Chicagoans. The lounge, called the Cuttysark, had a separate entrance.

As soon as I started working at the Goldcoast, I heard rumors that Mr. Sonken was mob connected. I figured I'd use what I'd learned growing up in Jersey City: work hard, make a living, and ignore the rest. Ernie, Joe's right-hand man, had worked for him for thirty-five years. Breeding English bulldogs was Mr. Sonken's hobby and pictures of his prize-winning dogs decorated the walls of the restaurant.

Sam and Sal, Joe's Italian troubadours, and I became fast friends. They went from table to table playing song requests for tips and had had their suit pockets enlarged to handle all the coins they got. I remember Joe forbade them to sing the Italian song "Momma." Before long, I began singing in the Cuttysark Lounge.

I worked there for two years. During that time, I even saved Sam's life. (For that story, read on.)

Man Down

When a man is drowning, you act.

Sam, one of the singing guitar players at the Goldcoast Restaurant, was a few feet way from me, flailing and screaming in the water. After countless times of maneuvering himself to his car without incident after a typical night of heavy drinking, he'd finally missed the turn. He'd dropped himself into the drink (so to speak). The worst of it was that he was definitely drunk. The next worst was that he was holding on tightly to his guitar in its guitar case and screaming: "My Guitar! My Guitar!"

The restaurant was on the intercoastal waterway. That night the tide was low, the moon was full and it lit up the darkness. I stripped down to undies and dove in. After surfacing, I barked at Sam to let the guitar go – that I'd get it after I got him. He didn't want to do it. His fear wouldn't let him. I repeated my order more sternly. After what seemed a long time, he released the guitar case and it quickly sank. Sam followed.

Luckily, I was close to him by then. I reached down, grabbed his collar, and hauled him over to one of the wood posts used for boat tie-ups. He clung to it, sputtering and miserable. The razor-sharp barnacles attached to the post prevented us from climbing up to the deck. Another serious problem was the upper arm strength needed to hoist our wet selves that far up – weight lifters we weren't!

Meanwhile, above our heads on land, a small crowd had gathered outside the bar and they were laughing and pointing at us. Furious, I shouted: "This is not fucking funny! Call Fire Rescue!"

I swam back for Sam's guitar and case. I found it quickly on the bottom where it had landed and felt relieved. Now the darn thing was even heavier it was so full of water. I struggled to haul it up before I ran out of breath. It dawned on me that maybe what I was doing was stupid, but I kept on anyway. Cursing all the way, I got back over to where Sam was.

I realized in my haste to save Sam, and after that save his beloved instrument, I hadn't taken off my Cartier watch. A prized possession, it had been a gift from my wife. Now I was really angry, but trying to control myself. Chewing Sam out at this time wouldn't have helped.

A few minutes went by. Sam and I cracked some lame jokes for distraction. Sirens blared, announcing the Fire Rescue team was (finally!) there. The collapsible ladder was thrown our way and we climbed up to safety. The drama was over.

Drenched, tired, and much too sober, we both dragged ourselves back to the bar and had another drink.

Years Later

I was reading a newspaper at a bar. An article captioned "Restaurant Owner Accidentally Drives Station Wagon into the Intercoastal Waterway" caught my eye. The photo showed a crane lifting Joe Sonken's car out of the same spot where I'd saved Sam! This time, it was Joe who was rescued. His two favorite bulldogs weren't as lucky. I'm sure he was heartbroken.

A Slight Disagreement

The hostile bellowing of the two East Coast mobsters had begun at the bar; then one had followed the other into the men's room. The bellowing got worse.

Then, along with it, we heard the sounds of heavy destruction. What could they be doing in there? Their other cronies continued to talk among themselves and eat. Just when Ernie, the manager, and I were positively sure no one would walk out alive, they did. They were soaking wet. Their beefy arms hung casually over each other's shoulders. They had big smiles on their faces. They said nothing. Neither did anyone else.

After a few long seconds passed, Ernie and I walked casually – our faces, masks of unconcern – into the men's restroom. We'd heard the incredible uproar. We'd ignored it as much as anyone could. But then water began flooding into the Cuttysark Lounge, streaming in from under the men's room door. The plumbing and the rest of the fixtures had been completely ripped out. Water was spraying in every direction! Incredible! We just gaped. Imagine the strength it had taken for those two to cause that much damage.

Soon, we quietly came out. We placed a few discreet calls to contractors behind closed doors. We said nothing.

Chapter 8:
Joyce and Me

A Real Beauty

Could that be Angie Dickenson? If not, she was still a beauty. I wanted to meet her and see if we had anything in common.

At a bar at the top of the Holiday Inn near the Miami airport is where I met Joyce, my Kentucky belle. She resembles Angie Dickenson and has a very quick wit. Joyce, a bartender, often said "anyone can make a drink; it's your personality that makes you a bartender." Easy for her to say, she had a great ass – still does, I'm sure. Joyce taught me the bartending skills I'm still using today. And that wasn't all she taught me.

On one of our first dates we went to see an X-rated movie starring Linda Lovelace. While the star did her thing up there on the big screen, Joyce said loudly, "I can do that!" The people around us laughed along with her while I tried to crawl under my seat…

The Cattlemen's Steakhouse Restaurant and Lounge in North Miami, operated by the Horowitz family, was where I worked the job I enjoyed most of any I've had. The Horowitz's partnered with Larry Elman of the NYC Cattlemen's. I was never ever bored working there. In a week, I was rotated as a waiter through the four theme dining rooms, the Western, the Casino, the Grand, and the Parlors of Madam Mustache. I also tended bar, covered for the maitre'd, and sang and played guitar when Allen, our entertainer took a day off. The regular customers enjoyed playing the "Where's Johnny tonight?" game. It was a standing joke. Plus, Joyce, now my wife, worked as a waitress there. She and I were quite a team.

When the Cattlemen's Restaurant closed, the Horowitz family opened Arthur's Eating House on 15th Street just off Biscayne Boulevard in the new State building. Then I worked there.

Donna, a breathtaking beauty, had been Arthur's "hostess with the mostest" when I had worked there. A former airline stewardess when model dimensions (36 – 24 – 36) were a job requirement, she later became the main squeeze of a rock and roll band leader. When she burned out on the constant traveling and the do-anything-and-everything lifestyle, she returned to Miami to thrill the rest of us. Donna would enter my life again years later…

Before the Iranian hostage crisis that began in 1979, many young Persian boys and men worked in South Florida's hospitality industry. I met Ali Shah, who was assistant manager, at Arthur's. Admired because he worked hard and had the determination to succeed, he was also genuinely likeable. He and I became buddies. We had all the same vices – drinking, gambling, and drugging. As far as trust between us, though, deep down we knew there wasn't much.

Living in North Miami with my three sons and Joyce's two daughters was quite the blended family. When Marion found out I was living with Joyce, she handed the boys over to me to raise. I eventually got a no-fault divorce from Marion and legal custody of them. Joyce and I lived together for 2 years before we married in a civil ceremony in 1973. From the time we met to when we divorced, twelve years passed. Joyce was my best friend and drinking buddy. Like my other marriage, this one ended badly. (Read on.)

Fights Won and Lost

My wife, Joyce, hit the Terrazzo floor hard. She had forced her way between the redneck and me after my first punch and gotten shoved roughly out of the way. (Note to Women: When your men are fighting do not get involved. Walk out! Leave them alone with their stupidity.)

This delightful evening had begun when Joyce and I had stopped for a few at a little dive, the 1600 Lounge, a neighborhood sports bar with a package liquor store and a couple worn pool tables. Joyce had just gotten off of work. The trouble had started innocently enough. I wanted to play pool. I found it relaxed me and I was pretty good at it. Just as usual, I placed a quarter on the pool table rail to show that I would challenge whoever won the current game of eight ball.

Joyce and I were drinking and chatting at the bar and I was monitoring the pool game to see when the game ended and my turn would come up. Joyce turned to me and quietly said "Let's go. I'm getting bad vibes."

I didn't listen. We'd barely started drinking and I wanted more fun. Ray, a guy I knew and who played at my level, had won the last game. I sauntered over and began the set up for the next one by plugging in four quarters to get the balls.

"What do you think you're doing?" The guy who'd lost the game, said. His blonde curly hair was evidently his pride. He'd grown it long on his head and wore his shirt buttons mostly open to reveal more on his chest. Hair: sign of a real man. He had three, young attentive women with him, I'd noticed. They'd served as his cheering section earlier.

While continuing the set up, I calmly replied: "You can see what I'm doing. I'm racking the balls to start a new game."

"You're not going to be playing any pool here," he said. I registered that he was much younger (10 to 15 years?) and bigger than me but I was getting pissed. I had waited a while by now and wanted to get on with a game.

"You ready to play me, Ray?"

"Yeah. Sure." Ray said.

After that, the kid says: "I repeat, you are not going to play pool here!"

"Why not? It's my turn," I replied. By now I have an edge in my voice.

"The reason you are not going to shoot pool is because I'm going to kick your ass from one side of this place to the other!" the kid loudly announces.

I've never seen this buffalo before and he's embarrassing me in front of my wife and friends. I got angry just thinking about him believing he could intimidate me.

* * *

Hey! Bartender!

My mind flashed back to an earlier situation I'd encountered as a teen.

Stuck recovering in a hospital bed in the Jersey City Medical Center, I had plenty of time to think. I tried to digest the life lesson I'd just acquired.

Not quite 16, I had a strong attraction for a little fox named Nancy at my school and let her know it. Being a looker, she, of course, already had a boyfriend: 19-year-old Herbie. He didn't like me hitting on his main squeeze one bit. For some days, being the studs we thought we were, we had traded threats using her as messenger. We were tough. Oh, yeah.

One sunny afternoon, feeling young, frisky, and free – tooling around in a black, Buick convertible – I saw Herbie walking on Ocean Avenue with some of his buddies. Rocky, the driver, pulled over to the curb. (First mistake.)

"Herbie! I heard we need to talk," I yelled. (Second mistake.)

I faced him, resting my arms on the car door, my chin on my folded arms grinning up at him, a naïve sucker – just asking for it. (Third and final mistake that day.)

Herbie strolled over, smiled a big sincere smile, and then hit me squarely in the left eye. Blood flowed from the gash he cut above my eye with a ring he wore. That first punch didn't begin to satisfy him, so he threw open the car door and pummeled me while I screamed, "Drive! Damn it! Drive!" to Rocky.

My buddy had frozen. He was sitting there, mouth open, dumbstruck. Then, realizing the mess we were in, he scrambled but couldn't get the car into drive. Scared shitless that the rest of Herbie's herd were going to come after us, he fumbled. Luckily, the guys stood back and watched, hooted, and yelled "Get him!" They saw Herbie didn't need their help.

Soon my little ol' handsome face was a bloody, puffy mess. One ear was cut badly and blood was all over the inside of my friend's beautiful car. The shirt I'd worn, one of my sexiest I thought, was ripped. Plus, I was in major pain. The next day I felt and looked even worse – the bruises and cuts began to display their finest colors. I couldn't see out of one eye and couldn't smile without grimacing for nearly a week.

Herbie had finished me off in less than 5 minutes with a continuous series of vicious punches. I had tried to cover myself, pulling my arms up over my face but whatever area I left unprotected, he hit. Surprised and humiliated, I was also deeply embarrassed. I vowed that never again would anybody take advantage of me that way.

* * *

The repeated threats this kid was making now triggered memories of that long ago humiliation and the vow I'd made. I spun around quickly from the pool table, ran two steps and punched the kid hard – a left hook to his mouth. He bellowed and blood gushed from his face. The place got quiet real quick. The kid backed up a step and Joyce ran over to drag me out of there. But no, I wouldn't go.

This was the point that Joyce decided real intervention was needed. She placed herself between us, which wasn't wise. She was soon flailing – shoved roughly out of the way – and then she hit the floor – really hard. I don't remember being at all concerned about her, due to my anger and alcohol haze.

Wiping the blood from his mouth, the kid yells "This is my blood! You cold-cocked me, you mother-f----er! You're a dead man." He charged at me and threw a couple punches. He swung so wildly they didn't land. Luckily, it appeared he'd had way too many beers and that was definitely in my favor. I hit him again, in the nose this time, and when it connected bam-on, it left an open gash. Now he was getting embarrassed and even madder.

His punches weren't working so he tried wrestling. As he grabbed me, I punched him in the left eye and then got him in a head lock. Some asshole decided to help the kid then and pulled my shirt up backward over my head. I couldn't see. I started struggling to get the shirt completely off.

Hey! Bartender!

I still managed, just barely, to hold the kid in the headlock and then he bit my knuckles. I roared like the wounded animal I was. I could just spy his rib cage from under my shirt and, thinking this might be my last shot, I hit him with an upper cut to his ribs. "Take that, asshole!" I cried. His scream after that is the one that I remember from the fight with real satisfaction. Since the whole match was pretty much over, some guys pulled us apart yelling "Break it up! Break it up!" like they had just become referees.

Some regulars who I knew only by face, held us. We were a couple of bloody, stinking, out-of-breath jerks barely standing up. I was calmer now, my anger spent, but the kid was still yelling and threatening me. I remember thinking: this buffalo is willing to fight till the death! Over what? A stupid pool game!

Joyce and I left. The others held down the kid so he wouldn't go after us. On the drive home, Joyce gave me the silent treatment. While I had "won," I had really lost.

With my bruised knuckles and gashes, I had gotten off easy. Joyce, meanwhile, had injured her tailbone when she fell. She couldn't sit for weeks! Her injury reminded us both daily of my immature recklessness. Looking back, I'd say this was the beginning of the end for the two of us. Now Joyce feared for her own safety when she was with me.

Did I mention she was also concerned about my effect on her daughters who were living with us then? One of my stepdaughters had referred to me as the "town drunk" one day (Ouch!) and since my life's philosophy then was "If it feels good, do it," Joyce was correct to be concerned. I was capable of just about anything.

We agreed that I needed to get out of the bar business for a while after I got fired from Morey's Meat Market – a place I hadn't worked for long. My next gig was driving a cab for the White Cab Company. I hadn't really realized what it took to navigate Miami Dad County with its many canals, bridges, railroads, and the river. I found it fun at first. Sure – I wasn't making much but I was drinking less and Joyce and I were getting along better. Weekend nights should have required hazardous duty pay for us cab drivers. I was now the one driving home people – whose car keys had been taken by a bartender or friend for their safety – after their all-night partying. My new view from the nearly sober side was not pretty.

When I received Joyce's 40th birthday present "How to Slow Down the Aging Process," it hurt my feelings. Me? Getting older? Ha! What a bitch she was to deliver the message to me that I was getting old. I calmed down a few days later and read the damn thing.

Today, I believe that book was instrumental in saving my life. While I still abused myself with alcohol and drugs, I ate better, exercised, and took nutritional supplements. I had become convinced the geriatric doc who wrote that book knew something. I was now an alcoholic, drug-abusing health nut.

And life went on.

Chapter 9: Long-Term Gigs

Stefano's

A five-minute, casual conversation between my wife, Joyce, and a woman named Pat started it. Pat, a regular customer of Joyce's at the New England Oyster House, was secretary to a restaurant operator named Stefano. Pat said he was partnering in a couple new restaurant/lounges that would open soon in Key Biscayne. (Stefano's opened in 1980.) She said Stefano needed an experienced bartender with a charming personality. Joyce told Pat she was describing me. Sometimes, you just had to love that woman.

Joyce and I had mutually decided that my hiatus from bartending should end. There had been a point where I needed to get away from that whole bar scene so driving a cab had made sense. Recent violent experiences I'd had while driving in the wee morning hours in Miami Viceville, had convinced us it was time for my second act. Though it involved alcohol and occasionally nasty fights, bartending usually didn't involve possible death. That's why, when the call to schedule the interview with Stefano came, I took it.

The interview was set up and the day and time for it finally came. Driving into Key Biscayne, the restaurant sat on the right side of the main intersection – a prime location. Not just a restaurant, the string of businesses that was Stefano's included a lounge, a disco, a liquor store, and a deli.

I parked, walked in, and found Stefano's office. Pat was there to greet me and asked about Joyce and our boys. We made small talk until Stefano got off the phone. From where I sat, I faced a wall of autographed celebrity photos, movie and sports stars mainly, with Stefano front and center in each of them. Before the meeting, I had asked around and learned that

Stefano had worked in California and the Bahamas before moving to South Florida. He seemed eager to meet me and his enthusiasm and confidence sold me immediately. The energy just radiated off of him – definitely that of a confident businessman. He said he'd grown up in the Piedmont region of Northern Italy and asked me where my family had lived originally. I answered "Basilicata." He smiled at my response.

Pat had told me that Stefano, unmarried with no children, was a few years younger than I. Joyce and I had practiced my answers for the range of possible questions he might ask. I had to contain my excitement.

We talked about what he needed in a bartender and what his plans were. I assured him I could handle the job. He asked about my experience in the local area. I had plenty. Shortly, I would discover that he'd hired a dream team for his restaurant staff. I knew I belonged. So did Stefano. He hired me. I didn't know this then, but his place, Stefano's – exciting yet comfortable – would be my primary environment for 14 years.

Stefano's took off quickly and became known for its northern Italian cuisine. Max, our French chef, prepared Fettuccini Valdostano and Shrimp Scampi that was so delicious our customers returned and ordered those same dishes repeatedly. My mother had prepared the rich, tomato and garlic-laden sauces of southern Italian cuisine when I was growing up but the northern dishes were new to my tastebuds. I brought recipes home, made them up, and impressed the boys. They hadn't known their father could cook!

Orlando, the host and assistant manager at Stefano's, had worked in hospitality for years, first as an airline attendant and then a cruise ship staff member. Pino, a service captain, was Austrian-born and added old-world European flair. His drive, talent, and business acumen later pushed him to own his own restaurant, The Towers of Key Biscayne.

Scene Changes

Stefano's ambiance, activities, and people changed throughout my shift – often nearly 12 hours long. Happy Hour specials kicked in at 5 p.m. We offered two-for-one drinks and delectable hot hors d'oeuvres. The joke was that everyone who lived on Key Biscayne had a realtor's license. During our Happy Hours this appeared to be an actual fact. The realtors and brokers making big money selling prime properties gathered at the bar then. I remember hearing them tell about the suitcases full of money their South American clients gave them to buy property.

After 7 p.m. dinner music began with the Joe Patrone trio or the BJ trio. Fine dining was an art with Stefano presiding as the gracious host, impeccably dressed, and smiling. He orchestrated exceptional service among his staff, making it look effortless, and encouraged everyone to have a good time. Did we!

Finally, at 11 p.m. until 5 a.m., Stefano's became a hot Latin disco. The most beautiful and talented Latinas chose our place to drink, dance, and flirt. Some nights, I wished the spectacle would never end.

Mostly though, by the time we heard "New York, New York" we were spent. After cleaning up a few of us would head to the Donut Gallery for breakfast fixed for us personally by Ben, the owner. He arrived at 5 a.m. to set up for the breakfast rush. His crew arrived later – at 7 a.m. I would order my usual: eggs over light, served with grits, sausage patty and rye toast. Also, we drank plenty of coffee. While eating, we'd sit and recap the night's events including who made the best cocaine score.

Using different room set-ups, subdued lighting, and up-tempo music the atmosphere would magically transform into a sizzling night club. Famous bands like the "New Love Band," the "George Tandy Band" and "China Valles" drew clients from the mainland as well as the locals.

Late nights, Stefano's was jammin'. Lines of the beautiful people snaked down the street clamoring to get in. No problem. Paying the cover was well worth it. You never knew which movie star or sports star you would spot.

Once you entered, shouting and hand signals became the best communication tools. The music was deafening. For the bartenders and other wait staff, these later hours became factory-like. We functioned as serving machines with no time for one-to-one chats. We did walk away with good money, though. Besides cash tips, our regulars would often share the wealth in other ways. By pouring a quarter gram of cocaine into a creased paper bill folded like an envelope and then discreetly palming it to you, for instance. These were known as "white bills." I amassed so much cocaine like this, I never had to buy it.

The drinks we often served had sexy-crazy names like "Slippery Nipple" (Bailey's Irish Cream with a Sambucca float) and "Screaming Orgasms" (a secret concoction I'll never reveal...). Favorites for their actual taste were Pina Coladas and Strawberry Daiquiris. I shuddered for those who hated themselves so much they went for Long Island Iced Teas. Do you have any idea what's in those? Well, let me tell you. Five white liquors are mixed: vodka, gin, rum, tequila, triple sec then a Coke splash, a sour mix splash, and a lime wedge are added. Yuck!

Our key hiring rules for waitresses were that they be young, beautifully built, and gorgeous. After they met this visual requirement, next came the questions: "Can you carry a tray of full glasses through sweating dancers and not spill a drop?" "Can you politely dodge passes from drunk men – some of whom come on to you like dogs?" Nearby the Church of Scientology and its followers held meetings. Several of our waitresses were scientologists. Maybe that philosophy helped them deal with the occasional poor mannered slob.

When the shift to digital music came, Stefano hired Carlo Sarli as our DJ. A problem had been that when the live bands took their breaks, the dancing stopped, and many customers would leave. Now this wouldn't happen.

Stefano often gave credit for his success to Fidel Castro for creating such a horrible environment in Cuba. In response, the wealthy Cubans fled to Key Biscayne where they could live well and enjoy his special place!

Dark Sides

The high life had its dark sides. Every week it seemed, a new tragedy would unfold. For instance, darling Shannon, our favorite bartender, died at 31 of liver failure. The only female bartender at Stefano's, she had grown up on Key

Biscayne and was proud of her "Key Rat" status. Shannon often fed the hungry raccoons that prowled around the dumpster out back of the restaurant. She was one sweet kid. We worked side-by-side so I got to know her well.

Our blond, good-looking relief bartender, Jack, from Boston committed suicide partly because he couldn't handle the severe pain of a chronic back problem along with other stresses. A drummer in our regular band, Tommy, a quiet guy, was shot in the stomach by his jealous wife. She believed he was cheating on her. She was probably right. One of our finest waiters, Emanuel, died a year after being diagnosed with HIV.

And then, too, we would hear about a shooting at another club and find out that one of our well-known regulars had been gunned down. Though this should have been sad and shocking, so many of us were anesthetized by drugs and alcohol we found it hard to feel anything.

Star Light

The Greatest

At the Fifth Street Gym In Miami Beach one afternoon, I had plopped myself on a bench to watch young Cassius Clay spar – always a thrill. The first time I saw him, I thought he was the finest specimen of a man I had ever seen! Many times I watched him box with Jimmy Ellis, his most notable sparring partner. As teens, Cassius and Jimmy met while training in the same gym in Louisville, Kentucky. Later, Cassius Clay changed his name to Mohammed Ali to reflect his change of religion. He won the world heavyweight championship in boxing three times and is widely considered one of the best boxers of all time. Ali's self-promotional skills were legendary. Jimmy went on to be a heavyweight champion, too, by the way.

When I first went to see Cassius train, he hadn't achieved full greatness yet so few other "groupies" were there. Later, the crowds would come. Alternating, each sparring partner would box three rounds with Ali. Most times, I'd watch 12 rounds of pretty damn good boxing. Some of the fighters would get pretty testy with him – he never stopped dancing or taunting his opponents while he boxed. He'd just wear them out.

Then, he would unleash some lightning combinations that would abruptly end the matches. This was still early in his professional career but he had already won an Olympic Gold Medal in the Summer Olympics in Rome in 1960.

This particular afternoon, a sideshow was about to begin. Some reporter had rigged up sound and lights and was preparing to conduct an interview with Clay. Since I was close, just a few feet away, I could watch it all and overhear every word.

The Champ, still sweaty after sparring, a towel wrapped around his neck, walked over to another bench and sat down. After the reporter introduced himself he said, "Please don't be nervous, Champ, it's just going to be a short, to-the-point Q and A..."

Ali bolted as if electrified. "What you mean tellin' me not to be nervous! I'm twenty-three years old and I have the United States government trying to put me in jail for draft evasion. I've got these hungry contenders trying to knock my head off to take my belt away. I've got wives suing me for money! And you tell me not to be nervous. There ain't another 23-year-old man in the world who has my kind of problems! So, I think you should be nervous – not me!"

The startled reporter didn't recover from the shock of Clay's tirade. The rest of the interview was lame.

The Fifth Street Gym had been cobbled together by brothers Chris and Angelo Dundee who had moved to Miami Beach from New York City. Italian-Americans born with the name "Mirena," they changed their last name to "Dundee" to honor a famous fighter with that name. Their gym occupied the second floor of a building at Fifth Street and Washington Avenue in Miami Beach. Previously, the space had been a Chinese restaurant. Angelo, who became Clay's trainer, jokes in "My Life from the Corner: A Life in Boxing" that he won high praise from his brother, Chris, for how much money he DIDN'T spend on getting the space ready for training the fighters. In the book's foreword, Muhammad Ali wrote that besides being a great trainer, "he (Angelo) let me be exactly who I wanted to be, and he was loyal. That is the reason I love Angelo." A crony supplied his famous motto "Float Like a Butterfly; Sting Like a Bee."

My Very Own Movie Producer

The glamour of Stefano's included the nonstop parade of entertainers and other high rollers you would meet there. One of my favorite customers, an Italian movie producer named Salvatore Alabiso, based in Rome, typically came to Key Biscayne for four months in the winter. When we met in 1984, I had been sober for about a year and was evolving into good friendship material. As the years passed, Salvatore and his beautiful German wife, Uta, would become a big part of my life. Our love of football, the National Football League (NFL) and betting brought us together.

Monday nights were the nights off for entertainers around Miami. Many of them would come in to meet their buddies so we'd drop down the big screen TV in the bar and get caught up in the football action. You couldn't call it a spectator sport with our crowd – we were all coaches! When it came to football, Salvatore couldn't learn enough. His questions seemed endless: Who's the favored team? What's the line? Any players injured? What's the spread? He quickly learned most of the rules of the game and how scores were kept. Soon the time came when he decided he wanted to place a bet. The usual bet among our group was $50 or $100. Not for him, though. Salvatore started with a $10,000 bet! (Plus the $1,000 for the transaction.) Whoa! I wasn't going to get in on this! This was way, way out of my league and I had sense enough to know it.

A recent hire who was working in Stefano's kitchen said he'd place the bet. He wanted the money put up in advance. So Salvatore went somewhere and came back with the money ($11,000!) in a paper bag. He gave it to the cook who placed the bet for him on the favored team.
They lost. (Ouch.)

The next weekend came. Undaunted by the previous week's loss, Salvatore placed $15,000 on the favored team in the game for that upcoming Monday. The same cook placed the bet. His team won! The whole place had cheered wildly throughout the game for his team. They were thrilled for him when it won. Unfortunately, this time, the cook ran off with the winnings…

Salvatore reacted calmly to this news. That just blew my mind.

When Salvatore asked me to spend a vacation in Monte Carlo with him and his family the following summer, I said "yes," knowing that sometimes plans like these don't work out. Still, the offer seemed genuine. Sure enough, the following June, I got the call asking me to visit for ten days in July. Hmmm. Should I go or not? That decision took me about 3 seconds!

By the late 70s, and early 80s, Salvatore became famous and wealthy for producing spaghetti westerns and slapstick comedies featuring two main actors, Terence Hill and Bud Spencer. Salvatore had been a regular Stefano's customer for some time when one day he and Stefano thought they'd have a different kind of fun. They cut a deal. Salvatore could use the restaurant in his movie "Super Cops of Miami" if the Stefano's restaurant marquee would be highlighted. Stefano's was closed for a day so scenes in the movie could be made. This was highly unusual. I was offered a role as an extra and I was, of course, secretly sure that someone would spot me as the next big star. (Right! If you look closely, you can almost pick me out in a few scenes.) They should have had me sing – that surely would have done it!

Another Day, Another Star

"You look an awful lot like Yogi Berra," I said to the man in the loud checkered suit.

"Everybody tells me that!" the man replied.

That man WAS Yogi Berra – so of course, everybody told him that!

As you may know, Yogi Berra was a very famous baseball player – a 15-time all-star who played for the Yankees beginning in 1946. He played in 14 World Series games. In addition to Yogi, the Yankees winning team came to include Micky Mantle, Roger Maris, "Whitey" (nicknamed for his white-blonde hair) Ford and others.

"Yogi" got nicknamed by a childhood friend because he thought his buddy looked like a TV actor playing the part of a Far Eastern Hindu spiritual guide or yogi. The nickname stuck. Besides being a star athlete, Yogi became known for his think-twice quips like "It ain't over 'till it's over," and "It's deju vu all over again."

Miami Dolphins' Head Coach, Don Shula

Don Shula, the extraordinarily successful head coach of the NFL's Miami Dolphins, often came in to have a quiet dinner with his wife at Stefano's. They would stop in on their way to the airport to fly to the out-of-town games. Don coached the Dolphins when they became the only undefeated team in the NFL's history. Being such a football fan, of course when I served them, I had to talk to Don about the most recent game. I remember how irritated his wife used to get with me for interjecting myself into their private dinner conversation. To her credit, she suffered my fan's enthusiasm and intrusion in silence. They probably never had a moment's peace when they were in public during the football season.

Another Big Fish, Larry C. Csonka

When I saw Larry, the famous Miami Dolphin fullback at Stefano's I stuck out my hand. I asked him how it felt to be "young, strong, rich, and famous." He laughed, shook my hand and said, "I wish God would bestow on me the ability to hit the urinal!" How can you not like a guy like that?

Paul Newman

Mr. Newman and Sally Field were in Key Biscayne shooting "Absence of Malice." During a break, Paul was checking out the wine selection in Stefano's package liquor section when I saw him. Always a guy to go with what works, I used one of my standard lines on him: "How does it feel to be young and handsome?"

He tightly clasped my hand and I'll never forget what he said. He looked me straight in the eye and said "Only in memory!" Then to counter the awkwardness of having revealed himself he laughed.

Mr. President, Sir

Having President Nixon's winter White House located on the island put Key Biscayne on the map. Several times, I served him and his friend, Bebe Rebozo, when they came to relax at the restaurant. Before President Nixon found Key Biscayne, it seemed no one had ever heard of it. I admit I had sort of liked it that way. Was this discovery by the masses really a good thing? I watched our island paradise become more popular and continue changing.

Donna and Me

"Donna is in heaven," her Mom said.

The breathtakingly beautiful woman with the radiant smile and bouncy personality whom I and many others had adored was gone.

Donna, the hostess at Arthur's Eating House when I worked there briefly, had been in a serious relationship back then. I was a mess and not fit for any kind of relationship but still in one with someone else, too. Dazzled by her, I convinced myself that she was unobtainable – for many reasons.

One night more than five years later, I saw Donna with friends at Stefano's. I was now free of alcohol and drugs and had new confidence. I had heard she was unattached and campaigned to get her to go out with me, calling her every so often and asking for a lunch " for old times sake." Finally, she agreed. Lunch led to dinner, and dinner led to my home. I serenaded her, singing and playing my best songs on the guitar. Kenny Rogers, Neil Diamond, whoever she wanted me to be, I was him!

She explained that she was living with a friend temporarily since she had moved out of her boyfriend's place. I saw opportunity here. I would coax her into staying with me, an old friend, for a while, just until she got on her feet again. Two days later she moved in with me! Of course, her poodle and kitten came, too. She adored her animals.

I had no idea what was coming. Physically, we fit well together. Donna loved sex and so did I. Sometimes sex can be more addictive than any drug known to man. Now that I was actually thinking about my behavior again – no more drug and alcohol haze – I considered whether I was using sex with Donna as my next addiction. Surely it was healthier?!

Long-Term Gigs

Traveling to England in March 1990 for our first trip outside the U.S. brought us closer. With mounting excitement, we made our plans. I had fun quizzing my English customers at Stefano's about where to go and what to see. Our lodging, the Beauford Bridge Hotel, was in Dorkin, thirty miles from London. After arriving at Heathrow, exhausted after the 7-hour-plus flight, we rented a car. I found out what it was like driving on the opposite side of the road. Confusing! Donna gave me grief about my poor driving performance until I had had enough and pulled off the road. I offered the keys to her. She got the point. I continued as driver, my skill steadily improving with each passing day. My humor improved after the jet lag wore off as well.

We hit the usual tourist sites: the Tower of London, Piccadilly Circus, Buckingham Palace, St. Paul's Cathedral. Another of our adventures was gambling at the Sportsman Club in Soho.

When we got home, Donna's drinking got worse. I attended Al-Anon meetings. That was cool. A recovering alcoholic seeking help because his significant other is a drunk. At the meetings, I had some role confusion, as you can imagine. When the attendees at these meeting shared their personal experiences they sounded like me – not just Donna!

Our arguments got wild and the police and the courts got involved. Break up. Get back together. Break-up. Get back together. "Fatal Attraction" and "Halloween" had nothing on us! Two years of this and we ended up deciding that Donna needed to go home to her parents and siblings in California. Maybe they would be able to help her. I felt terrible that I couldn't seem to encourage her to stay clean.

She did go home and I called her mom regularly for updates. I was saddened because I never received a good report. Not too long after that, her mother told me that she had died and mailed the obituary to me.

Donna had barely made it into her forties.

Chapter 10: Rock Bottom and Up

Snow in Florida

At a certain time in my particular semi-tropical paradise, it was snow, snow, and more snow – cocaine, that is. Coke was fast becoming the rage in Miami and South Florida and using it was a status symbol. Brash young professionals bragged openly about the quality of their snow. My longtime working buddy, Ali, (No. Not that one…) and I were in tune with the high life. Oh, yeah! We were players. Well, we were poker players…

One evening, during our weekly poker game at my house, a new guy, Roger, came and brought me a dubious gift: a new addiction. He pulled out a vile of cocaine, took a "bump" from a tiny gold spoon, and passed the vile and its contents around. Ali and I joined in – we were so cool. To us, it symbolized something. Coke wasn't a street drug – it was a designer drug for the elite who could afford the best. We had arrived!

Added to the unending amounts of alcohol I was downing (my drink of choice was vodka and water) I had no idea then how completely crazy I would become.

For five years, I heavily used both. The combo made me totally fearless. I would be driving home in the middle of the night, radio blaring, The Stones' "I Can't Get No Satisfaction" – high as a kite pretending to be a race car driver. Since nobody else was on the road, I used it as my private speedway. To stay on the road, I would keep the car's nose on the reflectors dividing the two lanes. Thank God I never killed anyone! I blew out three car engines this way. (The metal came through the oil pan and broke the camshaft.) I told Joyce the car was demonic.

Hey! Bartender!

Quoting my car repair guy: "Johnny! I've only seen this happen with race-cars! What the f---- are you doing?!!"

He had me there.

My life went from bad to worse. Rumor had it that Joyce was having a passionate affair with a young chef where she worked. I was furious. How dare she look elsewhere for love and happiness? While it was true I wasn't paying her much attention, still – I WAS her husband. I decided I wasn't going to kill just myself. I was going to take revenge on Joyce, and kill her, her young lover, and then myself. If she thought she could really leave me, she was wrong!

I had lost the battle with alcohol and drugs. Living with me at this time was my youngest son, Anthony. He witnessed me bottoming out. He listened to the scenarios created by my sick, paranoid mind that was filled with anger and hatred. I was in excruciating pain and wanted to die. It couldn't come soon enough for me. Today would be the day. I would do it myself!

A torrid, six-month, love affair with a very beautiful woman from years earlier flashed through my mind. Of course! I'll call Lynn! I was looking for any reassurance I could get. Surely, she'd take my side in this mess! I hadn't called her in years but our relationship had been truly unforgettable. She was a gorgeous ex-dancer working as a bar manager when we met. Joyce and I had just begun seeing each other and she had left town for a while to resolve some family business. I had been available, sort of. Lynn was ending a relationship with a live-in boyfriend back then. Later, when we split up, it had been because both that live-in boyfriend and her ex-husband had decided she and I should part. The message had come through loud and clear when my new rental Oldsmobile mysteriously blew up in her driveway one dark night.

Now Lynn told me sincerely that she was happily remarried. She told me how proud she was of her husband, David. She made it clear there was no chance for me with her. Still, she asked me to call her the next day so we could talk some more. I said I would. She made me promise, so I did. I called her the next day and the day after that. Sometime she even put her husband on the phone to talk with me. I found it weird. Here she and David would take time to talk with me, one of Lynn's former boyfriends, when everyone else I knew and saw was avoiding me like the plague.

I'm Saved

I called Lynn one last time, I don't even remember why. Then in my continuing craziness, I described my violent plans to her. She said: "I know who I am talking to now. It is time for you, Johnny." Then, after a pause came, "Repeat after me," and she led me through a short prayer. Afterward, she comforted me – telling me that I wasn't going to do any of the awful actions that I had threatened. She told me that drugs and alcohol would soon be taken out of my life.

Something happened to me when I talked with her. I listened to the goodness and calmness in her voice and it penetrated my soul. I saw and felt a flicker of light (was that feeling hope?). I had been suffering in complete blackness. From that conversation on, I no longer felt deep within myself that I was going to die a horrible death. Most importantly, I didn't want to die any more.

Lynn asked me if I knew of anyone who was Christian where I worked. "I think Alan is," I told her. Alan, an entertainer, was someone I saw most days. Lynn suggested I tell him that I had been "reborn" (her word). When I told him that night what had happened to me, his eyes popped wide. He embraced me warmly in an awkward but heartfelt bear hug. Then, he asked if I'd attend church with him on our night off, Wednesday. His sincere excitement caught me and I couldn't say no. (Me? Going to church?)

Before long, the cocaine went down the toilet, the drinking slowed down, and I was regularly attending church services at Good Shepherd in North Miami! I was a whole, new Johnny!

One sunny late afternoon not too long after that while driving to work I prayed that God would remove the desire for alcohol from me. I had dropped the cocaine habit already. However, it broke my heart when I learned that I would need to deprive myself of alcohol, too. If I was going to beat my demons I knew that half-measures would avail me nothing.

I didn't announce my decision to stop drinking to anyone for a full two weeks. I wanted to be certain that I could back it up with action. During that time, my withdrawal from alcohol made me truly miserable. Delirium tremens – and what felt like convulsions – took over my body. I rode them through.

As people started noticing my new behavior, they didn't know what to do with me because they didn't know who I was. I tried to tell them. They either didn't believe me or just didn't want to hear the truth. I went to Alcoholics Anonymous meetings – sometimes three per day just to hold myself together. With the loss of total anesthesia, I started to feel my emotions – the good ones and the uncomfortable ones. I felt lonely and rocked by deep fear.

When would it get better? I wondered.

Diane and Me

Now I was a church-going man, I was single again, and I met Diane.
When she shared a personal prayer with me that she had written to God asking for a Christian husband, I understood that I was meant to be that man. After our first few dates, we had gotten unusually close. My relationship with Joyce had been over less than 6 months at that time, plus I was still finding out who I was without drugs and alcohol. I was extremely lonely and vulnerable.

Diane, divorced with three mostly grown children, had been sober for 5 years. She worked tirelessly as a chef and counselor in a private Christian school. I remember baking pizzas from scratch with the students. They loved that. Diane's life goal was to become an ordained minister serving a large congregation. Later, she would achieve this.

Diane also headed a ministry for those with addictions at Good Shepherd and that's how I met her. I started attending the group each week. She welcomed me immediately and actively involved me by having me play guitar and sing hymns and contemporary Christian songs. I had never sung any

Christian songs before. Songs that I picked up fairly easily and memorized were "I Have Decided to Follow Jesus,""He is Lord – He is Lord," "We Are One in the Spirit, We Are One in the Lord," "Come Let's Glorify My Lord," and "Jesus, Jesus in the Morning, Jesus in the Noon Time." Others hymns I sang from sheet music. Always Mr. Hospitality, I served coffee and donuts at the weekly meetings.

I was grateful for Diane's close and careful guidance through my early recovery phase. She taught me what she'd learned through her own recovery experiences. I learned a lot from her. As time went on, though, I recognized that she had not followed the basic rules that are given in AA, such as no major life changes for a year after you initially stop drinking. In some ways, I felt betrayed and that eroded the trust between us.

We also had friction in our home between our youngest sons who were both actively using alcohol and drugs. We acknowledged the situation between them was dangerous and could spin out of our control. We talked the issues through with our friends at church and determined we'd made a mistake when we'd married so quickly. Our relationship ended.

Married and divorced in a year – a new record for me. This time, I promised that I would take a full year for myself – without jumping into a new relationship. It proved to be a year of real growth.

What I learned was that sobriety had to be the most important thing in my life. An alcoholic without sobriety has no life worth living. I knew that. I needed to choose an experienced sponsor who would guide me through the twelve steps of Alcoholics Anonymous (AA). I had been a misguided drunk for the better part of my life and was now adapting to the AA way of living. This entailed working the 12 steps to the best of my ability and practicing their principles in all my affairs. Early on, I often went to AA meetings two and three times a day to get the emotional support I deeply needed. For me, this led to tremendous spiritual growth. I was projected into a new dimension of life – as if I had been re-born. This has been the most precious gift of my life.

I now will go to any length to not ever touch another drop of alcohol. Amen!

Chapter 11: Roommates

Two Dudes and Two Dogs

During my growth year, my life got better and better. Stefano asked me once during this time, if I had changed my religion. I answered "no." Then I told him I would make up for any wrongdoings that had occurred previously while I had been working for him. He smiled and then confided that our profit percentage at the restaurant had gone up since I'd quit drinking. We were two very happy businessmen.

Then I discovered I was living with a convicted murderer.

Enzo, the quiet, polite, Sicilian friend who shared my house with me – was a murderer? Unbelievable!

When he first revealed to me that he had this dark secret, believe me, I had questions. One was: who is this guy? (I thought I knew him!) The next one was: what were the circumstances surrounding the murder? And finally: is he a threat to me, my family, or my friends?

Despite my shock, he told me the details. (Why is he telling me now? I wondered, when no one in his current life knew?) When Enzo was 17, he had killed another teenager in a gang fight. For this crime, at the age of 18, he was sentenced by the state of New York to die in the electric chair. He went on to explain that he'd served a total of 35 years in prison, 12 of them on death row. When the capital punishment law was declared unconstitutional, his sentence was changed to life in prison. Enzo studied law and constantly wrote to government officials using what he'd learned to plead for his release. Finally, he gained it – he was let out due to a legal technicality related to the pre-trial publicity his case had received.

Hey! Bartender!

After Enzo was free, he found the outer world a bewildering place. So much had changed during all those years he'd spent serving time. He knew he didn't want to return to New York to live. He moved to Miami instead and found a job as a maintenance man at the Sonesta Hotel, located across the street from Linda B's. He kept a low profile. I met him when I worked at the Cattlemen Restaurant, where May, his long-time girlfriend waitressed. He often came in to see her. Younger than he by many years, she had been a dancer and was still quite lovely. Besides chatting with him casually at the restaurant, I knew him from our weekly poker games.

I answered an unexpected knock at my door one night to find Enzo waiting on the porch in despair. "May kicked me out. I think it's over between us," he said. "I have no where to go."

I quickly brought him inside and told him he was welcome to stay with me for a couple weeks or even longer if need be. Instantly, relief flooded his face. He thanked me wordlessly, grasping my two hands in his. I could see tears in his eyes. My three-bedroom, two-bath house was way too big for me and my basset hound, Luke, anyway.

As the two weeks turned into months and then years, we joked about being roomies and household patterns developed. I worked nights and felt good about having the house occupied by Enzo then. My neighborhood had changed – and not for the better. Enzo's dog, Frannie, a mixed terrier, arrived with Enzo, so Luke got a buddy, too! It was "Love me: love my dog" for each of us and luckily we both did.

Enzo loved gardening and since my yard was big, he put in a vegetable garden. Fairly soon we were enjoying the fresh lettuce and tomatoes he had grown. Of course, he grew fresh basil and it flavored many of the Sicilian dishes he cooked.

Due to the yard having been designated a pet cemetery by my boys, we had to select a garden spot that was free of beloved pet remains. How many dogs, ferrets, cats, hamsters, parrots had the boys buried back there? By then, I'd lost count.

After we'd lived together awhile, one morning I went into the garden where Enzo was tending his tomato plants to ask him a question. After answering it, he said, "You know somethin' John? I'm happier today than at any other time in my life!" He was 75 by then.

During the following three years of his life, Enzo had progressively worse problems with the way his heart functioned. The doctors implanted a defibrillator which extended his life. However, after suffering many near death experiences and associated recoveries in the local hospital's intensive care unit, he decided he was ready to go. He died at age 78. I lost a good friend.

Chapter 12: Alcohol

Management

Open Minded

"I'll go. Who knows? I might learn something," I said.

Darling Gina, Stefano's secretary, looked surprised. Johnny volunteering? I was the only bartender from Stefano's who said he'd go. I guess the others thought they knew everything about bartending already... Lately, I had felt myself becoming more open to new ideas. Before I changed my life, I would have blown a seminar off, too.

How bartenders can help prevent alcohol-related injuries and accidents – that was the topic. Too many people die from alcohol-related mistakes. We all know it. Taught by a former beverage manager/bartender, Mr. Johnson, the six-hour educational seminar had been produced by a few major liquor manufacturers and distributors. Mr. Johnson opened the seminar by showing a video of white-coated docs. They stated that bartenders sell and distribute a legalized, controlled drug. The fact that the government regulates its manufacture doesn't change its effect on people. Liquor is so commonplace (like aspirin) that most of us don't really think of it as a potentially dangerous drug. The audience members, mostly bartenders, were encouraged to take their role in preventing injuries and accidents seriously. Mr. Johnson stressed that bartenders have a responsibility to their customers to help them handle themselves when they're under the influence. A little known fact was thrown in about George Washington being a successful whiskey distiller. (Drinking – a part of our national heritage!)

The seminar continued and just got more and more interesting. Based on five real case stories, a series of videos were shown. Different endings demonstrated how bartenders could change problem situations as they were developing for the better. In one scenario I remember, a group of people were drinking at a table for several hours. The server gave them as many drinks as they requested. She never slowed their drinking nor did she alert the bartender to the situation. When some of the people at the table began to argue loudly with each other, they were all told to pay their check and leave. They did. Later, just a couple miles down the road, they had a car accident — no one survived.

Using the same actors who had played in the previous film, they showed how, using different techniques for serving, the waitress and bartender could have prevented the accident.

This seminar revolutionized my approach to bartending.

I learned to count the number of drinks that my clients consumed – keeping in mind that it takes about an hour for the body to metabolize one ounce of alcohol. Also, alcohol metabolizes better when food or snacks are eaten. When I notice clients drinking too quickly and excessively, I approach them and ask if they are driving. This question alone often checks their consumption.

By far, the most difficult task for a bartender is having to tell clients they can't have any more to drink. Arguments and threats often follow. The two most valuable sentences I have ever learned for successful bartending are: "Sir or M'am: In good conscience, I cannot serve you another drink. Should anything ever happen to you from me continuing to serve you, I would not be able to live with myself."

I actually had a man cry when I said this to him. He said, " I don't believe how much you care about me. No one has ever shown me this concern before at a bar. Thank you, thank you, thank you. I will not have any more to drink this evening." Now that's what I'd call a positive outcome!

Communications between the bartenders and waiters is key as well. Working as teams, they can monitor for excessive drinking at the tables and decide whether to intentionally stay away to slow down the drinking pace.

Men in Black

"Bartenders are supposed to sell drinks, guy. So keep serving 'em!" the well-dressed man said. One of four black suits, probably lawyers I guessed, sitting at a table, he was shooting shots of tequila and Irish coffee so fast I couldn't keep up with him. Nor was I going to try.

"Whoa! What's this? You tryin' to kill yourself? I said.

"If you had just gone through what I went through, you'd act like this, too!" he said.

"So, what happened?" I asked.

"My wife is filing for divorce and as of today, we're legally separated. I have no visitation rights with my kids. I have to pay hefty child support and alimony. And I'm losing my house!"

"Wow!" I said. "What do you do for a living?"

"I'm a lawyer."

"Guess what," I replied. "If you continue to drink this way you're going to lose your license to practice as well."

Now he became more puzzled.

"Aren't you a liquor salesman?" he said.

"Not if you could be hurt by it," I answered and I meant it.

I saw him again at our bar about a week later. He was slower with his drinking. He wondered if it had been me who had put the AA info he'd found inside his suit jacket pocket. I admitted it was. Then we really talked.

I gave him "AA When and Where" a leaflet that tells where the AA meeting locations are. I didn't see him again for months. Then he popped in one day to tell me his good news.

91

Hey! Bartender!

"Hey, Johnny! I'm now in AA and my life is going better. My wife and I are talking and I have visitation rights with my kids."

Later, I heard from someone that he'd started a new AA group for young professionals and that he gives credit to "a little Italian bartender in Key Biscayne" for getting him straight.

A man walks into a bar… and gets sober! Huh?!

About this time, Stefano underwent a big life change, too. He met his future wife Linda, a beautiful and talented Texan, at the Turnberry Isle and soon married her at that same special place. The Miami Herald covered their wedding with a full-page spread. Life was good.

Stefano was so successful, he opened other restaurants. One of them he named after his new wife: Linda B. Steakhouse. For short, we called it "Linda B's." Stefano had given in to my request for a transfer from Stefano's, so I went to work there. I enjoyed the change to the quieter fine dining environment and the more mature clientele.

Chapter 13: The Fall

Invaded

Business was slow that day – a couple regulars sat lounging at the bar and a few elderly people were picking at their early dinners in the main dining room. I was checking bar stock, part of my routine before my official shift, and had one ear listening to the early evening news. I had just come off the tennis court with a win after a close game and was feeling OK.

Suddenly, the front doors burst open, and crashing through the entrance came five policemen in camouflage-colored riot gear holding shotguns and automatic rifles. A guy in civilian clothes ran in just after them.

I was surprised and angry.

"What in God's name are you people doing? You're scaring everyone to death!" I shouted. I ran out from behind the bar. The guy who seemed to be the leader strode up to me with a scowl on his face. John, a regular customer and an attorney, was sitting at the bar. He quietly suggested I ask if he had a search warrant. I did. No response. He demanded to know if Linda, the owner, was on the premises. I said "no." He asked to see the headwaiter. He wasn't in either. I told him that.

"Well, who IS in charge here? the guy barked.

"I guess I am," I said. Now that they had had their effect, he told the SWAT team to wait outside. Then, he drew his badge out and showed it to me. I read that he was a federal agent. After that, he pulled out a paper that showed me that he did have a search warrant. My fear level went up several notches.

Whatever was going on, it was clearly serious business. I told him I would cooperate and he quickly asked for the "keys to the house" – meaning every key the restaurant had. I took them out of my pocket and immediately handed them over. In minutes, a few new plainclothesmen had entered the office and were briskly hauling books, files, and computers out to a van in the front driveway. Everyone in the restaurant felt invaded. Early on, the senior agent turned to our restaurant guests and apologized. He suggested they finish their meals. They stayed in their seats and did as they were told. Though they seemed shocked and scared at first, I'm sure it was mighty entertaining – if you were a disinterested party, that is! I decided not to present them with bills. (Wasn't that the least we could do?)

It crossed my mind that maybe someone was going to yell "Cut" and we were going to find out Linda B's had secretly been chosen as a movie site. But no – the strangeness continued. A couple hours were spent in buzzing activity with the local news crew reporting next to me at the bar. We tried to remain calm as we watched ourselves on TV. It got very weird.

Having a cop as my eldest son, and having heard his real life horror stories, I wasn't as shocked at the drama as some were. Still, it was intimidating. My tough old heart continued beating wildly.

Thank God I knew I hadn't done anything wrong.

Aftermath

"Crime and Nourishment" and "Miami: See It Like a Drug Dealer" blared headlines in the Miami New Times. These news stories filled in details about the Linda B's raid and other key investigation findings. Stefano and Linda had become local, well-loved celebrities in Key Biscayne by this time (the late 90s) and many of us were shocked when this federal crime was exposed.

The story goes that an employee introduced Stefano to an Italian who was supposedly representing a drug cartel syndicate. What Stefano didn't know was that the man, Vinicio Avegnano, was a government informant. Extensive film and audio recordings were being made of their meetings. When Avegnano made a 14-million-dollar offer to Stefano for all his assets, he accepted. The irony was that Stefano had made it known that he was totally against drug use. The feds targeted two of his restaurant staff members, the headwaiter, at Linda B's and the chef at Sundays on the Bay. Dealing cocaine on the side from the restaurants, their activities were used as the excuse for the feds to wade in deep and investigate Stefano's many businesses. The raid at Linda B's where I worked occurred in August 1996.

Albert Krieger, who had served as mafia boss, John Gotti's high-profile defense attorney, was hired to defend Stefano and Linda. His skill and connections helped get bail for Linda in less than a week. As a U.S. citizen, she wasn't viewed as a flight risk. Stefano was. He held Italian citizenship so his bond was set quite high. Still, relatively soon, he too was out on bail. While they awaited trial, they operated Linda B's and most of us stayed on. Their notoriety seemed to have improved business and, strangely, they relished the public attention they were getting.

Both were facing 20 years in prison if convicted of conspiracy to launder drug money. After about a year, in 1997, they were convicted. The upshot was that Stefano's, Sundays on the Bay, Linda B. Steakhouse, Salty's at Haulover Park, and Bellini's on Captiva Island were confiscated.

To avoid the lengthy sentence, Stefano struck a plea bargain. In it was 5 years probation (no jail time) for Linda and a 7-year prison sentence for him. Afterwards, he was to be deported.

I felt sad that my friends had been brought down in this way. At the same time, I was relieved that I had not been involved.

Chapter 14:
More Recent
Years

Marcia and Me

Originally from Havana, my friend Marcia's father, Ruben, had relocated the family to Puerto Rico to escape Castro's rule, and then later they moved to Key Biscayne. I had been told that her father was a son of the ex-president of Cuba. Younger than me, and much prettier (!) Marcia was divorced with two young daughters. She worked as head teller at the local bank on the Island.

Marcia loved to dance – especially salsa – and she was a fantastic dancer. During the time we dated, Ruben had a serious stroke which meant her mother Josephina, became his fulltime caretaker. Other family members helped but for the two years he lived I observed the sacrifice and love she showered on her husband and was deeply impressed. What a kind, loving person she was.

Finally, I realized my chance with Marcia had come. Alina and Marcia (two beautiful Latina cousins) were at Stefano's drinking at the bar together – no boyfriends! They were unattached, they said. Marcia had been in a steady relationship when I'd first met her. I had been dazzled even then. We connected and had such fun together we talked about marriage. Then we did more than talk. Marcia and I got married, each for the fourth time, at her house with immediate family attending. We then left for Key West to honeymoon. The next day, Marcia said something odd "that she didn't feel like she wanted to be married." What?! Now what would happen?

What happened was: disaster struck! Hurricane Andrew struck our beautiful paradise. We lost power during the night and it didn't come back on for almost two weeks! We had no TV and so had little idea about how severe the damage was. Having seen the devastation on their TVs, concerned relatives from Puerto

Rico and others parts of the U.S. called to see if we'd survived. Brian Norcross, the weatherman, had reported that not a single home or building could have escaped the effects of Andrew. This stunned me. I had been living through hurricanes for more than 35 years and nothing had come close to this!

Cold showers, eating food cooked on the outdoor grill, using candles for light at night, playing cards – these were our main family activities. We were lucky though, because we had prepared and had ample, food, water, and supplies. Marcia's girls were still young enough to view this as one big adventure. Of course, no school was in session because it was summertime. Very little damage was done to Marcia's house. Mostly the roof required repair. The place was quite sturdily built. Again, we were lucky.

Marcia and I were together for many years. We broke up. We stayed friends and continued to see each other.

Key Islander

"What do think, Johnny?" Tom asked.

I was silent for a minute or two. I hadn't expected this. I continued washing bar glasses and tried to gauge how I felt about the idea.

"I'll think about it," I said.

"You do that!" Tom replied. He paid for his Dewars on the rocks and left soon after. Tom had shared his dream of owning and operating an Inn in Maine. (This sounded like a nightmare to me; I hate the cold!) Now he saw how to make it happen. First, he would have me take his place as building manager of the Key Islander Apartments.

During the course of the next few weeks, I tried to think of reasons why I shouldn't do what Tom thought I should but I couldn't find any.

That's when I committed to becoming: "El Jefe de Edifice" (the building manager). The job description was the kind I loved: you're independent and do anything and everything to make the place function well. I would use my outgoing personality, leadership skills, electrical and maintenance skills, and my well-honed hospitality skills. In addition, I'd gain other skills I hadn't ever dreamed I'd have such as computer skills.

Tom and I had met when Marcia and I were on the outs and I'd needed a rental in a hurry. The Key Islander was one of the few apartments left on the island, so it had been one I'd considered. Luckily, the owners allowed pets because my dog and I needed a new roof over our heads – pronto! Tom leased me a one bedroom and we became fast friends. From him I learned that the Key Islander offered some unique features. First, the ground floor was dedicated to vacation business. People rented apartments on that floor by the week. Second, the two upper floors were leased annually. Since the absentee owners lived in Dublin, Ireland, Noel, the controlling partner needed a trustworthy person on-site, though he visited Key Biscayne regularly, mixing business and pleasure.

Bless Tom. For six months, he trained me and had the patience of Job – especially when it came to the computer training I needed. From not knowing anything, (I mean absolutely nothing!) Tom brought me along gradually until I could use the reservation program, answer e-mail inquiries, and do the basic bookkeeping. I had plenty to learn about licenses and insurance, too. He had some meltdowns when my lack of computer skills caused mysterious crashes but I learned to make myself scarce at these times. We had plenty to do – in and out of the office – and after some months I mostly overcame my lack of knowledge and skill with continued practice. I remember the first time Tom showed me how to get on the Internet – it opened a new world to me.

Noel and I came to terms on my salary and he said commissions would be paid when I successfully rented out weekly rentals. Now I just had to figure out how to balance my work at Linda Bs and the Key Islander. Peak season that first year was wild and I promoted each place when I was working at the other. That strategy paid off. When summer came, the schedule lightened and I could enjoy my life in paradise a little more.

The day came when the building's numbers hit a new record for annual sales. Our little team was proud. Noel agreed to reinvest some of the profits in apartment upgrades. I had pushed for them because it was time – the apartments had a somewhat run-down appearance – and I wanted to be proud of my building. Pedro, who had worked maintenance, had many trade skills that we began to use more fully. Pedro and I picked a weekly rental to upgrade as a sort of pilot project. We wanted to clearly show the owners the improvements that we could make at a relatively low cost. In each apartment, we planned to gut and remodel the kitchen and bath and tear out the carpets and tile the floors. For extra pay, Pedro handled the floor work. This switch to tiles made maintenance much easier for our residents who dearly loved their pets – no matter how old and leaky they became. We completed the remodeling by installing new furniture.

We dazzled the owners and got the go-ahead to remodel the rest. A new helper for Pedro enabled us to remodel the remaining weekly rentals. We really had fun. Presto Chango!

* * *

One day, arriving at Salvatore's home to enjoy my regular lunch date with Salvatore and his wife, Ute, I was pleasantly surprised to discover a lovely young woman visiting, too. (Marcia and I had by now amicably divorced.) Gladys spoke no English, only Spanish, and was visiting her sister, Leticia, who was Salvatore's housekeeper. Gladys and her family came from San Pedro, Honduras. I knew immediately that I wanted to date Gladys. I asked Letitia to please translate my interest into Spanish words Gladys could understand. Gladys agreed on the spot and we decided to go to the Miami Seaquarium on our first date.

With the pocket translators from Office Depot I'd purchased at the ready, we had fun attempting to communicate through words and phrases. It was a workout but "love was in the air" and "where there's a will there's a way". These sayings do mean something, after all. We laughed and shared what we could. Romance bloomed and after several trips home to Honduras and back Gladys agreed to come and live with me in Key Biscayne. Earlier, she had told me of her desire to become a U.S. citizen and I was, of course, happy about that.

We married.

* * *

When my Key Islander housekeeper, Martha, gave notice to take a private housekeeping job with a wealthy family, it seemed to make sense that Gladys take her place. The timing was right, Gladys needed work to do, I could trust her, and she'd need no transportation. Also, her inability to speak English would pose no problem. The job would give her a start in her new country.

Our lives were rolling along well. I was pleased with just the two of us snug in our little place. Then one morning, I got one of the bigger surprises of my whole life.

"My two sons are arriving at Miami Beach airport today. They will be coming to live with us." Gladys stated matter-of-factly during breakfast.

"What?!" I shrieked. I quickly grabbed my pocket translator to ensure my communication to her would be crystal clear. "You could have told me in advance about the sudden increase in our family," I punched in. What kind of game was this? Had I been had? My emotions were all mixed up. I was hurt and furious and felt used. This was the way our relationship was going to go? I hadn't even been asked if her sons could join us? – just informed – at the very last minute?!!

Gladys calmly reminded me that she had talked with me about the boys. I then vaguely recalled a conversation we'd had awhile before about her wanting my help with her sons, Giovany, 12, and Rene, 10. I tried to adjust to the upcoming situation. What choice did I have?

We located the boys in the international terminal and they gave their mom hugs. I was introduced. They nodded and each boy shook my hand somewhat formally. First, I asked if they were hungry. They were way too excited to care about food. I went to get their luggage. I knew what parents did.

They stared at the strange people, the shops, and commented on all the choices. They even stared at me when they thought I wasn't looking. We walked to the car and stuffed their belongings in first and then climbed back in the car for the ride home.

"Do you have a computer and a CD burner at your house?" the twelve-year-old asked. He was so earnest and excited I was glad I could answer "yes".

Hey! Bartender!

As I drove, Gladys was busy pointing out buildings and gorgeous Miami Bay and the Seaquarium where we had had our first date and saw the "pesces grande" (big fish). She could feel how angry I was. Her ploy was to distract the boys and me with nonstop chatter – like a guided tour operator. The boys were all eyes and very quiet. So was I. Gladys just kept on talking.

Meanwhile, I had to deal with my feelings and thoughts. How could she have done this! Two more sons for me – just like that. I was 65. Furious still, I tried to talk myself into the situation. When we got home, I looked at them closely: good-looking, well-mannered, needing a home. Nearby Key Biscayne Elementary would be their school. They could walk there, it was so close. I adored their mother and she wanted them with her. They'd be safer with us to watch over them. Also, the opportunities they would have in the U.S. would enable them to fulfill much more of their potential. Within hours, I'd talked myself into Dadship once again. Hey! I was used to having boys around. Maybe things would work out.

Recruited immediately for the soccer team, Giovanni and Rene were popular at school in no time. My friends told me to my face that I was totally nuts to take on a new family. Hadn't they noticed my life-long condition before now?!

At about this time, I switched sports from tennis to golf. Arthritis in my left hip had forced a replacement surgery – tennis wouldn't be fun anymore – just work and pain. When the Coconut Grove K-Mart held a going out of business sale in which they offered golf clubs for three dollars a piece, I started buying. I assembled a learner's set of clubs, bought myself a golf bag, and began hitting balls at the driving range every day. Dennis, a neighbor, and I played (if you could call it that) and he informed me that it would take three years to get good at golf.

Then and there, I promised myself that I would beat him at golf in 18 months. An overheard conversation between Dennis and I led to my current job as a ranger on the golf course. Paradise is mine!

As time passed, and the boys became teenagers, our lives got more difficult. We decided to divorce and stay friends. We did and we have.

Chapter 15:
My Life Now

Living My Golden Dream

As I ride around in my golf cart in the beautiful sunshine, a slight breeze plays over my face. The woman friend sitting beside me is enjoying herself, too. The temperature is in the 80s. Here at Crandon Golf Key Biscayne, a favorite place, there's plenty of time for me to think. It's quiet; peaceful. As a ranger, it's my job to help keep the golfers moving along, so everyone can enjoy playing. My reward is getting to play this challenging course, the third most challenging public golf course in the U.S. per Golf Digest, by the way, for free. My golfing buddies include Tony, Edgar, Sergio, Marcello, Dave and his wife, Rita, Maryanna, Dick, and Daisy. We play often and we're getting better and better.

I see nature's beauty all around me. Iguana's stalk the course. Frightening and strange-looking at first, you get used to seeing them basking in the sun. Fish, turtles, and alligators live in the water traps. Overhead, you'll hear the squawks of both parrots and seagulls and you can see out into the bay and across it to the Miami skyline.

I ride my bike through "my private beach" in the mornings during the weekdays when hardly anyone else is there. Often, I walk in the bird sanctuary nearby and watch the Ibis and other birds enjoying themselves. Who knew it could be fun to watch baby peacocks eat lettuce leaves?

My three sons and my grandkids call me on my cell to catch me up on their latest doings. My two stepsons, now grown, and my ex-wife, Gladys, who is still a good friend, stop by sometimes.

Hey! Bartender!

Singing in the church choir, going to Bible study, and attending services at Key Biscayne Presbyterian Church is a joy. I just donated my old guitar to the church for use in the contemporary service. Now, I use the Ovation guitar my eldest son, Jay gave me to accompany myself when I sing the hymns and Dean Martin and Neal Diamond songs that I love.

I'm still bartending. This keeps me connected with many long-time customers and friends like Susan, Marielda, Peggy, Tom, and Albert. The list could go on, but I must stop somewhere!

Finally, I feel grateful that I'm still here enjoying every day. And I think, "Hey! I'm living my golden dream! After all, I hate the cold."

Johnny's Favorites

Authors
1) God and the Disciples (The Bible)
2) John Grisham
3) Tom Clancy
4) Bill Wilson (co-founder of Alcoholics Anonymous)

Movies
1. "True Lies"
2. "Don Juan Del Marco"
3. "Amadeous"
4. "Chariots of Fire"
5. "Some Came Running"
6. "Gone with the Wind"

Bible Verses
1. 2 Timothy (1-7)
2. John (1-5)
3. Psalms 23 and 150

About the
Authors

Johnny Catanio

Dared by many people to record the events of his dramatic life, Johnny, who thrives on challenges, wrote the first draft of Hey! Bartender! a few years ago. It wasn't easy! As a successful businessman in the hospitality industry, Johnny's thrilled to be living his golden dream in Key Biscayne, Florida. Johnny's sincerely happy to share this finished book with you. If you really want to know more about him, he suggests you read this book!

Patricia Alma Lee

A Chicago author, editor, and writing coach, Pat works with successful businesspeople to coauthor or edit books and e-books that offer original knowledge and important stories. Recent works include: "A Life Less Anxious," "Speak Your Truth," and "Clinical Preventive Medicine." Pat founded a writing program for veterans at the Pritzker Military Library. She also co-teaches "What's Your Story?" a writing and publishing course. She wrote, produced, and starred in "A Soldier's Tale." Pat has written extensively for web sites and publications at the Feinberg School of Medicine at Northwestern University, the Rehabilitation Institute of Chicago, and the American Medical Association. A University of Illinois graduate in English, Pat also completed the University of Chicago's Publishing Program.

Amanda Catanio

A native of Key Largo, Florida, Amanda graduated from Norwich University in the Corps of Cadets with a B.A. in Studies in War and Peace and an English minor. This year, she achieved a master's degree in Nonprofit Management and Leadership from Walden University, while working at the Pritzker Military Library. Engaged to Laurent Felizardo, Amanda is planning a June 2011 wedding. The couple will travel in South East Asia with the Elijah Foundation before pursuing their dream of founding an orphanage in the Philippines.

Thank You All

Thank you to the entire Catanio family and their friends for their many gifts to me.

Thank you to my employers and co-workers who have made – and still make – working such a pleasure.

Special thanks to Lynn for saving my life and giving me the opportunity to become a whole new Johnny! Thanks to Joyce for putting up with me all those years and to Marcia who helped me mature. Most of all, I thank my Lord and Savior, Jesus Christ.

Pat thanks her husband, Ray, her three sisters, Sandy, Elizabeth, and Kristie, and her father, Don, for being loving and supportive in her creative endeavors. She also thanks God for everything!

When You Visit Key Biscayne

You must:

1) go to the Seaquarium, see the shows, and get wet! Be sure to sit close to the front!
2) visit the lighthouse and read about our island's history and growth.
3) slow your pace and enjoy the natural beauty surrounding you and give thanks for another day full of opportunities for love and laughter.
4) Come by to see me and say "Hey! Bartender!"